Decentralized Applications
Harnessing Bitcoin's Blockchain Technology

Siraj Raval

Beijing · Boston · Farnham · Sebastopol · Tokyo

Decentralized Applications

by Siraj Raval

Copyright © 2016 Siraj Raval. All rights reserved.

Printed in the United States of America.

Published by O'Reilly Media, Inc., 1005 Gravenstein Highway North, Sebastopol, CA 95472.

O'Reilly books may be purchased for educational, business, or sales promotional use. Online editions are also available for most titles (*http://safaribooksonline.com*). For more information, contact our corporate/institutional sales department: 800-998-9938 or *corporate@oreilly.com*.

Editor: Tim McGovern	**Indexer:** Judy McConville
Production Editor: Colleen Lobner	**Interior Designer:** David Futato
Copyeditor: Octal Publishing, Inc.	**Cover Designer:** Randy Comer
Proofreader: James Fraleigh	**Illustrator:** Rebecca Demarest

August 2016:   First Edition

Revision History for the First Edition
2016-07-13:   First Release

See *http://oreilly.com/catalog/errata.csp?isbn=9781491924549* for release details.

978-1-491-92454-9

[LSI]

Thank you, Jade. Your truth set me free.

Table of Contents

Preface

Conventions Used in This Book

The following typographical conventions are used in this book:

Italic

> Indicates new terms, URLs, email addresses, filenames, and file extensions.

`Constant width`

> Used for program listings, as well as within paragraphs to refer to program elements such as variable or function names, databases, data types, environment variables, statements, and keywords.

`Constant width bold`

> Shows commands or other text that should be typed literally by the user.

`Constant width italic`

> Shows text that should be replaced with user-supplied values or by values determined by context.

Using Code Examples

Supplemental material (code examples, exercises, etc.) is available for download at *https://github.com/oreillymedia/decentralized_applications*.

This book is here to help you get your job done. In general, if example code is offered with this book, you may use it in your programs and documentation. You do not need to contact us for permission unless you're reproducing a significant portion of the code. For example, writing a program that uses several chunks of code from this book does not require permission. Selling or distributing a CD-ROM of examples from O'Reilly books does require permission. Answering a question by citing this book and quoting example code does not require permission. Incorporating a significant amount of example code from this book into your product's documentation does require permission.

We appreciate, but do not require, attribution. An attribution usually includes the title, author, publisher, and ISBN. For example: "*Decentralized Applications* by Siraj Raval (O'Reilly). Copyright 2016 Siraj Raval, 978-1-4919-2454-9."

If you feel your use of code examples falls outside fair use or the permission given above, feel free to contact us at *permissions@oreilly.com*.

Safari® Books Online

Safari Books Online is an on-demand digital library that delivers expert content in both book and video form from the world's leading authors in technology and business.

Technology professionals, software developers, web designers, and business and creative professionals use Safari Books Online as their primary resource for research, problem solving, learning, and certification training.

Safari Books Online offers a range of plans and pricing for enterprise, government, education, and individuals.

Members have access to thousands of books, training videos, and prepublication manuscripts in one fully searchable database from publishers like O'Reilly Media, Prentice Hall Professional, Addison-Wesley Professional, Microsoft Press, Sams, Que, Peachpit Press, Focal Press, Cisco Press, John Wiley & Sons, Syngress, Morgan Kaufmann, IBM Redbooks, Packt, Adobe Press, FT Press, Apress, Manning, New Riders, McGraw-Hill, Jones & Bartlett, Course Technology, and hundreds more. For more information about Safari Books Online, please visit us online.

How to Contact Us

Please address comments and questions concerning this book to the publisher:

O'Reilly Media, Inc.
1005 Gravenstein Highway North
Sebastopol, CA 95472
800-998-9938 (in the United States or Canada)
707-829-0515 (international or local)
707-829-0104 (fax)

We have a web page for this book, where we list errata, examples, and any additional information. You can access this page at *http://bit.ly/decentralized-applications*.

To comment or ask technical questions about this book, send email to *bookquestions@oreilly.com*.

For more information about our books, courses, conferences, and news, see our website at *http://www.oreilly.com*.

Find us on Facebook: *http://facebook.com/oreilly*

Follow us on Twitter: *http://twitter.com/oreillymedia*

Watch us on YouTube: *http://www.youtube.com/oreillymedia*

## CHAPTER 1

What Is a Decentralized Application?

A new model for building massively scalable and profitable applications is emerging. Bitcoin paved the way with its cryptographically stored ledger, scarce-asset model, and peer-to-peer technology. These features provide a starting point for building a new type of software called *decentralized applications*, or *dapps*. Dapps are just now gaining media coverage but will, I believe, someday become more widely used than the world's most popular web apps. They are more flexible, transparent, distributed, resilient, and have a better incentivized structure than current software models. This is the first book that will help you to understand them and create your own.

Preliminaries: What Is Bitcoin?

Before we get into the details of dapps, let's talk a little about Bitcoin and the Web. We've seen the Web grow considerably, by orders of magnitude, over the past decade. Billions of people are coming online as Internet-connected device distribution expands globally. At first glance, the standards of communication set in the Internet Protocol Suite seem to be working well enough: the Link Layer puts some data on a wire; the Internet Layer routes the data; the Transport Layer persists the data; and the Application Layer delivers abstractions of the data in the form of applications. All four protocols work together seamlessly for exchanging data, but not value. Bitcoin acts as a fifth protocol layer for value transfer that lives up to the standards of the other four.

We do have an existing way of sending payments on the Web. The problem is that they all involve inefficient legacy systems like Automated Clearing House (ACH) that were designed before the Internet. These traditional payment systems are painfully slow because they require a centralized clearing house. Machines shouldn't have to wait days for a payment to clear; they are constantly communicating with one another. They should be able to send billions of micropayments to each other to meter resources like electricity and storage space and not have to worry about the hefty transaction fees of a middleman. Bitcoin helps solve this problem.

With the advent of Bitcoin, instant, decentralized, pseudonymous value transfer is finally possible. Bitcoin's anonymous creator, who used the assumed name Satoshi Nakamoto, effectively solved the *Byzantine Generals Problem*, a problem that had plagued cryptographic research for decades. To quote from the original paper (Lamport, 1982) defining the Byzantine Generals Problem: "[Imagine] a group of generals of the Byzantine army camped with their troops around an enemy city. Communicating only by messenger, the generals must agree upon a common battle plan. However, one or more of them may be traitors who will try to confuse the others. The problem is to find an algorithm to ensure that the loyal generals will reach agreement." Achieving decentralized consensus in Bitcoin meant that no longer did one party have to go through a central authority or trust the other party to share information, including information in the form of value transactions.

Bitcoin and other cryptocurrencies will help define the fifth protocol layer of the Internet, letting machines transfer value as fast and efficiently as data. Bitcoin is a useful tool for online value transfer, but its most valuable innovation is its underlying technology, the *blockchain*, that for the first time in history made decentralized consensus possible.

The blockchain is a massively replicated database of all transactions in the Bitcoin network. It uses a consensus mechanism called proof-of-work which prevents double-spending in the network—a problem that had plagued cryptographic researchers for decades. Double-spending meant a bad actor could spend the same funds twice, denying the first transaction happened.

Proof-of-work solves this problem by having *miners* in the network solve cryptographic proofs using their hardware. Miners are Bitcoin nodes that verify a transaction and check it via its blockchain history, a timestamped record of all transactions ever made in the network. Someone could theoretically alter their blockchain history, but with proof-of-work, they would also need to have the majority of computational power in the network to verify it. Because the Bitcoin network has much more computation power at this point than all of the world's supercomputers combined, an attacker would have an extremely difficult time trying to break the network.

Proof-of-work is expensive in terms of the cost of electricity and compute workload but it's the only known prevention mechanism against Sybil attacks, in which a bad actor claims to be multiple people in a network and gains resources that they shouldn't by doing so. A successful Sybil attack on the Bitcoin network would most likely result in a complete devaluation of the currency because people would no longer trust its stability. As expensive as proof-of-work is, it's the only thing that's proven to work so far on a massive scale.

So, we have this new tool called the blockchain, a massively replicated database of transactions that's able to avoid Sybil attacks. For the first time, the blockchain lets us achieve decentralized consensus without the use of a centralized server. You might be wondering what use cases this would have, and rightly so. I'm going to be devoting a good portion of the book to helping you think about all of the possibilities and ways with which you could implement them. The important bit for now is to understand that this data structure is one of many that will help you to create profitable decentralized applications.

What Is a Decentralized Application?

Most people are familiar with the term "application" as it pertains to software. A software application is software that defines a specific goal. There are millions of software applications currently in use, and the vast majority of web software applications follow a centralized server-client model. Some are distributed, and a select few novel ones are decentralized. Figure 1-1 shows a visual representation of these three models for software.

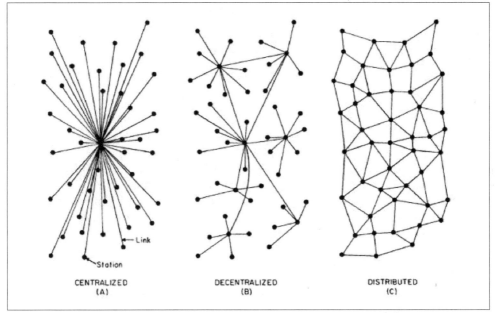

Figure 1-1. The three different types of software applications

Centralized systems are currently the most widespread model for software applications. Centralized systems directly control the operation of the individual units and flow of information from a single center. All individuals are directly dependent on the central power to send and receive information and to be commanded. Facebook,

Amazon, Google, and every other mainstream service we use on the Internet uses this model. Let's call these huge services "The Stacks." The Stacks are useful because they provide a valuable service to us, but they have immense flaws that I'll go into in Chapter 2.

So, what's the difference between decentralized and distributed?

Distributed means computation is spread across multiple nodes instead of just one. Decentralized means no node is instructing any other node as to what to do. A lot of Stacks such as Google have adopted a distributed architecture internally to speed up computing and data latency. This means that a system can be both centralized and distributed.

Can a system be both distributed and decentralized?

Yes, it can. Bitcoin is distributed because its timestamped public ledger, the blockchain, resides on multiple computers. It's also decentralized because if one node fails, the network is still able to operate. That means that any app that uses a blockchain alongside other peer-to-peer tools can be distributed and decentralized.

Then, why isn't the title of this book Distributed and Decentralized Applications?

Centralized systems can be distributed as well. Software applications that are able to achieve decentralized consensus are a real innovation.

So, is having decentralized consensus the only requirement to being a decentralized app?

The dapp space is currently an emerging field with a lot of smart people still experimenting with new models. Different developers have different opinions on what exactly a dapp is. Some developers think that having no central point of failure is all it takes and some think that there are other requirements. The focus of this book is to talk about profitable dapps; that is, dapps from which developers and users can earn money. The reason for the profit focus is because profit is the cornerstone of a successful, robust, and sustainable dapp. Incentives keep developers building, users loyal, and miners maintaining a blockchain. To that end, Figure 1-2 shows the four features any profitable dapp should have.

Feature 1: Open Source

Decentralized, closed-source applications require users to trust that the app is as decentralized as the core developers say it is, and that they don't have access to their data through a central source. Closed-source applications thus raise a red flag to users and act as a barrier to adoption. The aversion to closed source is particularly pronounced when the application is designed to receive, hold, or transfer user funds. Although it might not be impossible to successfully launch a closed-source decentralized application, the battle would be uphill from the start, and users would favor open source competitors. Open sourcing a dapp changes the structure of its business practices so that the Internet is common denominator instead of a chain of closed silos.

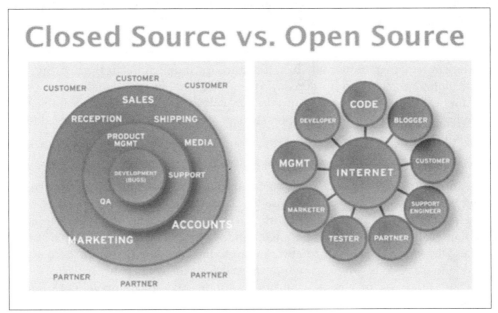

Figure 1-2. Closed source versus open source business plans

Any app can be open source. So why aren't they?

If we delve into the traditional business models, all of them require the product or service for sale to be better than that of the competitor. Open sourcing your product would mean that any competitor could take all of your work, white label it, and sell it as their own.

So, what incentive is there for app developers to open source the work from which they plan to profit?

Bitcoin is a good example of an open-source dapp from which the creator profited handsomely. Satoshi kept an initial amount of Bitcoins and let others use the rest. Because Bitcoins were limited in quantity and the network itself provided huge value to society in the form of its novel proof-of-work mechanism, the value of Bitcoin started to increase and so did his wealth. Having the app be open source made it possible for the network to achieve the transparency it needed to improve itself with developer contributions and grow trust among its users to give its coins real-world value. Open sourcing your dapp will gain the trust of potential users. Anyone can fork your dapp, but they can't fork your development team. Users want to get behind the people best suited to maintain the dapp, and often, those people tend to be the original developers.

Feature 2: Internal Currency

A question that consistently comes up in dapp circles is how to monetize a dapp. Traditional modes of monetization for centralized applications include transaction fees, advertising revenues, referral commissions, access rights to user data, and subscription services. If you open source your dapp, how are you supposed to make money? You might try programmatically inserting a fee for transactions in the network that would automatically go to the app developers' account, but that would rely on trusting users to not fork the app and take out your commission—not ideal. Neither is embedding advertising, subscription services, or any of the other centralized business models.

How is any open-source dapp developer supposed to make money?

The answer is to allocate scarce resources in the network using a scarce token: an *appcoin*. Users need this appcoin to use the network. Owners of scarce resources get paid in appcoins. In the Bitcoin network, the owners (miners) of the scarce resources (computing power) are paid with transaction fees directly from the users so that they can use the service. Because the network grew to include more users and there were a fixed amount of coins from the outset, the values of the coins grew, as well. We can apply this model to any kind of dapp. Scarce resources could be storage space, trades, images, videos, texts, ads, and so on.

Does this mean users would need to pay to use any dapp?

Yes and no. Although blockchains are pay-to-play, there are different ways to structure incentives within dapps. Users could receive a sign-up bonus of coins or even have the option to willingly sell their data or local storage space in exchange for coins. Besides using appcoins, dapp creators could monetize virtual assets like real estate in a decentralized MMORPG, domains in a special namespace, or even reputation.

Feature 3: Decentralized Consensus

Before Bitcoin, consensus on transaction validity always required some degree of centralization. If you wanted to make a payment, your transaction had to go through a clearing house that monitored all transactions. Bitcoin is peer to peer (P2P), which means nodes are able to talk to each other directly. P2P networks are not a novel thing; Distributed Hash Tables (DHTs) like BitTorrent were invented before the blockchain. DHTs are great for storing and streaming decentralized data, but if you want application-level constructs like usernames, status updates, high scores, and so forth for which you need everyone to agree on in a decentralized way, you'll also need a blockchain. The blockchain doesn't replace the need for DHTs, but it does serve to complement them. What makes the blockchain unique is that it solves the major security issue of DHTs: not forcing nodes to trust each other on the validity of data. The blockchain is a decentralized database of transactions and it's the first decentralized database that is highly tamper-resistant. The blockchain's security was a domi-nant design goal. It is the first ever organizationally decentralized and logically centralized transaction log. Here is a map of what I mean.

	Organizationally centralized	Organizationally decentralized
Logically centralized	Paypal	Bitcoin
Logically decentralized	Excel	Email

The blockchain's innovation is decentralized consensus. If your app needs some feature that requires everyone else to agree on something, you should use a block-chain. A simple example is a username system for which it doesn't really matter who has the "@user" username; what matters is that everyone agrees who has it. There have been lots of decentralized protocols in the past, but they all required nodes to trust one another. The blockchain is an immutable record that every node has a copy of, so no one can pretend that they too are @user. This can be done via the use of *smart contracts*.

A smart contract is a piece of code that lives in a blockchain. When a preprogrammed condition is triggered, the smart contract executes the corresponding contractual clause. You might be thinking, "What makes that different from doing something like this with Stripe's API?"

```
if (user.sendsMoney(customerID))
{
runContract();
}

func runContract()
{
 println('hello world');
}
```

One big difference: smart contracts live on a blockchain, not a server. No third-party trust is required, and there is no need to trust Stripe or a server owner. So, a more formal phrase for smart contract would be a "cryptoeconomically secured execution of code." One thing to keep in mind is that not all dapp code is a smart contract, and although smart contracts have their own specific use case, for the purposes of this discussion they will generally act as one "model" in a model-view-controller dapp architecture. We'll talk more about that in depth when I begin walking through dapp architecture.

Feature 4: No Central Point of Failure

Dapps can't be shut down, because there is no server to take down. Data in a dapp is decentralized across all of its nodes. Each node is independent; if one fails, the others are still able to run on the network. There are a number of decentralized database systems on which to build dapps that allow for this feature, such as Interplanetary File System, BitTorrent, and independent DHTs.

The History of Decentralized Applications

In its early days, the Web was obviously not as useful as it is today with the array of apps and services that do everything under the sun, but it did have a more DIY distributed feel to it. The Web was pretty decentralized from the outset. The HTTP protocol connected everyone on the planet with a computing device and an Internet connection. In the HTTP protocol guidelines, there are a set of trusted servers that translate the web address you enter into a server address. Furthermore, HTTPS adds another layer of trusted servers and certificate authorities. People would host personal servers for others to connect to, and everyone owned their data. But soon, application servers began taking off and the centralized model of data ownership as we know it today was born. Why did it happen this way?

The simple answer is because it was easy, both conceptually and programmatically. It was the easiest thing to do and it worked. One individual or group pays for maintenance of a server and profits from the users that utilize the software on it. Apps like MySpace and Yahoo! were among the first popular centralized apps. More recent apps like Uber and Airbnb decentralize the "real-world" parts of a business by providing a central and trusted data store. They are among the first to allow for participation in one moneymaking endeavor from all sides of the economy. Their decentralized business model foreshadows the development of even more decentralized apps.

As the HTTP web grew larger, a new protocol was introduced by a developer named Bram Cohen, called *BitTorrent*. BitTorrent was a protocol created as a solution to the lengthy time to download huge media files via HTTP and as an improvement on some of the P2P proposals before it, like Gnutella, Napster, and Grokster. The problem was that downloading huge files took a very long time and as the Web grew, so did the size of files that were available. Meanwhile, hard-drive space was increasing and more people were connected. BitTorrent solved this by making downloaders into uploaders, as well.

If there was a file you wanted, you would download it from not one, but multiple sources. The more popular the file, the more users who would be downloading it and subsequently uploading it, which meant you would be pulling from multiple sources. The more sources, the faster the download. Seeders were rewarded with faster download speeds, whereas leechers were punished with limited speeds. This tit-for-tat system of transferring data proved to be very useful for large media files like movies and TV shows.

BitTorrent grew and is for many the de facto way to download any sort of large media file like a game or movie. BitTorrent's speed, resilience, and reward mechanism proved to be better than HTTP for large data sets.

So, why doesn't the Web work this way?

Most likely because of HTTP's first mover advantage, its infrastructure, and all of the time and money already invested in it. There are currently active projects working on upgrading the HTTP web with BitTorrent-like technology, and they'll most likely be successful because of BitTorrent's huge value proposition. As soon as BitTorrent was introduced, developers began to use the technology to create nonprofit decentralized applications. Let's look through just a few examples of recent decentralized apps.

PopcornTime

PopcornTime uses the BitTorrent protocol to stream videos between users in real time, kind of like a Netflix for torrents. It is the worst nightmare of the Motion Picture Association of America (MPAA). No regulator can shut it down, and now everyone has access to free movies. PopcornTime proved to be a useful dapp acting as a decentralized version of Netflix. The creators claim that it has been downloaded in every single country, even the two without Internet. PopcornTime uses no internal currency and doesn't need decentralized consensus, so it had no use for a blockchain. It simply streams movies and that proved to provide a lot of value.

OpenBazaar

OpenBazaar aims to be a decentralized version of Ebay. No middleman can tell sellers what they can and can't sell or decide on the fees for using the service. It's built on the BitTorrent protocol, but the problem is that the sellers must host their own stores. They need to have their own server and leave it on in order for users to be able to see their items. Ideally sellers could just upload their store data to the network, perhaps paying a small fee, without having to worry about it. This requires a decentralized system of incentivized storage miners, which we'll cover in detail in Chapter 4. OpenBazaar uses BitTorrent's protocol for data transfer and Bitcoin as currency for transactions between sellers.

FireChat

FireChat emerged with a famous use case—the 2014 Hong Kong protests for democracy. China's infamous "Great Firewall" is notorious for blocking IP addresses for content that it deems prodemocracy or just not in its interest. The protesters feared the government would try to shut down access to various social networks to stop collaboration as is possible to do with the HTTP protocol. Instead, they used FireChat, an app that used a new feature in iOS 7 called multipeer connectivity makes it possible for phones to connect to each other directly without a third party. Because it had no central point of failure, the government would be forced to manually shut down every node, and thus the protestors were able to communicate with one another robustly.

Decentralized rebellion at its finest.

Lighthouse

We'll discuss Lighthouse in detail in Chapter 5, but it is a Bitcoin wallet embedded with a series of smart contracts. These smart contracts help pledge money to certain projects just like Kickstarter. When the project goal has been reached, it becomes possible to retrieve the funds out of the project backer's Lighthouse wallet. Pledgers can undo pledges at any point without the involvement of the project creator. Lighthouse is a great example of using the existing Bitcoin infrastructure to build your dapp. It is just a UI with some Bitcoin smart contracts built in as a wallet. It works and it builds off Bitcoin's existing user base. It has decentralized consensus, it's open source, it has no central point of failure, but it doesn't issue its own currency; rather, it uses Bitcoins. It's a useful dapp but it's not profitable for the creator.

Gems

Gems is a social-messaging app that is trying to create a more fair business model than WhatsApp. Gems is issuing its own currency and letting advertisers pay users directly with it for their data rather than acting as the middleman who profits. Users can also earn gems by referring others to the network. Gems are a meta-coin built on Bitcoin that developers also receive for developing and maintaining the software. As the Gems user base grows, so does the value of the currency. Users are incentivized to grow the network and earn money just like the developers. You can think of Gems as shares in the dapp. Gems hasn't open sourced its code, so users can't verify if they truly have no central point of failure. It's a profitable app, but in my opinion it isn't robust enough to withstand competitors who fulfill the other three criteria.

So, are there any standalone dapps that satisfy all four criteria: no central point of failure, issue their own internal currency, have decentralized consensus, and are open source?

There are plenty of cryptocurrencies that satisfy all four criteria, but cryptocurrencies aren't dapps. I'm talking about decentralized social networks, ride sharing, search engines: taking The Stacks and decentralizing them. The answer is not yet. It's possible, though—the technology exists, and as soon as a few emerge, a flurry of developers will jump on the decentralized bandwagon to make some serious money for both themselves and their users. Let's talk about some of these enabling technologies.

Enabling Technologies

I've already mentioned many of the enabling technologies during our discussion on the history of decentralized applications. Bitcoin's blockchain is, of course, of primary importance, so we'll take a deeper dive into this before considering the other enabling technologies. The blockchain helped solve the Byzantine Generals Problem. That problem asks the question, "How do you coordinate among distributed nodes to come up with some sort of consensus that is resistant to attackers trying to undermine it?" The proof-of-work algorithm and the blockchain help solve this.

When Bitcoin was created, decentralized consensus became possible. Proof-of-work isn't perfect—it is both computationally and energy expensive. There are alternative cryptocurrencies out there that solve meaningful problems, like PrimeCoin, whose miners use their compute resources to find prime numbers. In a world where Bitcoin is the de facto currency, we're going to be using a lot of energy to maintain the network, energy that could be put to better use than just helping the network maintain itself.

The problem is that proof-of-work is the only known Sybil-prevention system thus far. Consensus research is still ongoing and has not stopped with proof-of-work, but for now it's the best that we have. In terms of up-and-coming competitors to proof-of-work, there is a big one that comes to mind: *proof-of-stake*. Proof-of-stake isn't perfect, either, but it can complement proof-of-work.

Proof-of-stake is a consensus mechanism that relies instead on computational power to prevent Sybil attacks on stake in the network. Usually, by stake it means amount of cryptocurrency owned by the miner. The idea is that the more cryptocurrency you have, the more invested you are in ensuring the stability of the network and the less likely you are to perform a 51 percent attack to fork the blockchain. Delegated proof-of-stake is an innovation of proof-of-stake where a set of 101 delegates can vote on block generators. Both delegated proof-of-stake and proof-of-stake are still undergoing research, but if either proves to be secure in the long term, they could be used to complement or maybe even completely replace proof-of-work.

Defining the Terms

So why the term dapp? Why decentralized app? Why not Decentralized Application Organizations or Decentralized Autonomous Corporations or Decentralized Application?

The cryptocurrency space is saturated with differentiating terms for this theoretical and partially implemented ecosystem of dapps. The best way to dive into why I've chosen the term dapp is to dive into all of the existing terms for dapps and see what they're all about. Let's begin with dapp itself.

Decentralized applications (DAs)
> *Decentralized Applications* is the name of this book. I could've just as easily chosen DO or DAO or DAC. Why dapp? Because the common word in all of the phrases is "decentralized." Decentralized apps are the superclass of all decentralized entities that involve software.

Decentralized organizations (DOs)
> A DO is one that empowers all of its employees. The term doesn't really apply to the tools the organizations use; it's more a description of how it's structured. There are varying degrees of decentralization, and complete decentralization isn't necessarily the best way of doing things. In a traditional organization, there is a rigid, hierarchical structure of command.
>
> A decentralized organization gives voice to its employees and the power is spread more evenly among everyone. Company practices and milestones are made auditable by everyone and can be stored in a decentralized storage network for optimal resiliency. Humans don't need to be the only ones making decisions: smart contracts can take on roles like paying people by a certain date. DOs don't need to be based in a certain city, either; members can be spread out globally. In some systems (for example, Bitcoin), collusion is seen as a bug. In a decentralized organization, collusion is a feature. In the political realm, we call decentralized power democracy. We're seeing some startups recently opt for a more decentralized structure, especially as remote collaboration tools like Slack and GitHub progress.

Automated agents (AA)
> AAs don't need to mean SkyNet or some general artificial intelligence. We've had automated agents for at least a decade. AA just means a piece of software that runs without any human intervention; in other words, autonomously. A perfect example would be a computer virus. The developer made it and released it to the wild. It then decides to self-replicate or carry out any other maintenance algorithm with which it was encoded. Another example would be a daemon. A daemon is a program that runs as a background process in an operating system, like an email program. Automated agents have their ups and downs, they don't require any maintenance, but having unchecked agents can lead to an uncontrollable source of possible danger for humanity—more on that in Chapter 6.

Decentralized autonomous organizations (DAOs)
> This was actually what I was originally intending on calling the book before switching over to dapps. DAOs are just like DOs except AI makes the decisions, not humans. The protocol lives in a decentralized stack and doesn't heed any legal bindings. Humans aren't in charge, they are on the edges. AI is what makes the decisions and the DAO maintains itself. DAOs aren't just defined by having AI make all the decisions, they also have their own internal capital.

In short, each of these is a subclass of dapps, and a DAO is a dapp with AI controlled decisions and humans on the edges. Collusion isn't treated as a feature as in decentralized organizations but instead as a bug. Bitcoin is an example of a DAO.

Decentralized Autonomous Corporations

This one is controversial. Some think that this shouldn't even be a phrase because the word corporation is derived from the legacy system of legal contracts and hierarchical centralized control from which we are trying to evolve. The other side of the argument is that a DAC is a subclass of a DAO that pays dividends to its members. I am going to side with the former argument because I don't like the term corporation and if a DAO wants to implement dividends to its human and/or machine members, it can as a DAO, not a DAC.

So we've talked about dapps, DOs, DAOs, AAs, and DACs with an example of each. Let's take a look at Figure 1-3 to help make things a little clearer.

I like this chart a lot because it puts into context everything we've been talking about thus far. We're not at a stage yet where we can make AI (the holy grail, as the chart puts it), but we are at the next stage of evolution where we can begin making DAOs.

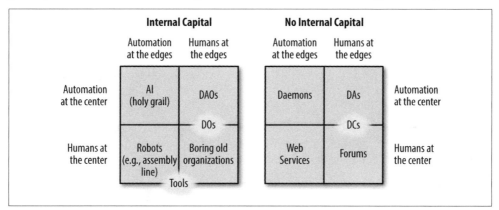

Figure 1-3. Types of organizations (Credit: Vitalik Buterin)

For brevity's sake, we're going to be using the term dapp throughout the book. Because dapps are the superclass of all decentralized software, and I'm going to be discussing different tools you can use as well as methodologies to define your dapp, you are best suited to decide what type of dapp you want to create.

My definitions have been pulled from my research from the cryptocurrency community, and my aim isn't to put yet another label on concepts or to create new paradigms. In fact, my aim is to simplify the space as much as possible such that you can fully grasp all the tools at your disposal to create a profitable decentralized app. The centralized app space has been nearly exhausted of ideas and it's time to iterate again after seeing its pros and cons. Dapps are the next wave of software and hopefully this book will prepare you to be a part of it.

Getting Started

I hope I've given a sufficient introduction as to what a decentralized application is. Much is still to be explained but this should've given you a brief introduction to the space and all the terms and acronyms associated with a dapp. My aim for this book is to first give you an explanation of dapps, what they are, why to build them, and what a thriving dapp ecosystem looks like. Then, I'll explain ways that you can implement your own using tools that currently exist. Finally, we'll take a deep dive into a few major players in the dapp space.

## CHAPTER 2

A Flourishing Dapp Ecosystem

The blockchain space can be pretty confusing. There is a seemingly endless array of startups, altcoins, ideologies, and buzzwords floating around, and it can be difficult to make sense of it all. It's useful to subdivide the space into three categories, following Melanie Swan's book *Blockchain* (O'Reilly) and others; blockchain 1.0 is currency, blockchain 2.0 adds in contracts (stocks, bonds, financial assets), and blockchain 3.0 encompasses applications beyond pure finance in areas like governance and health (dapps). In this chapter we're going to be talking about what needs to happen for all three to progress. As a dapp developer, you just want one thing: the right tools to make your dapp secure, robust, and profitable. This chapter will describe what a flourishing dapp ecosystem would look like; that is, an ecosystem where making dapps is really easy. I'll also discuss the technical requirements to make a dapp and what is currently possible.

There are four concepts in web applications that have traditionally been in the domain of centralized control: identity, wealth, data, and computing. Each of these requires trust in a provider—a trust that can be betrayed. Recent advances in distributed-system technology can put users in control of these things, so let's dive into these enabling innovations step by step.

Decentralized Data

This is the most important of the concepts to me. Currently, we trust "The Stacks" with our data. We willingly give them our data for free in return for a free service. Or, we pay them to store our data—but we only have enough data to make that worthwhile if our users are giving us *their* data for free! We trust that they won't misuse and sell our data to entities to which we would rather not be exposed. Since Edward Snowden, we now know that trust can, has, and will be broken as long as we entrust our data to a central entity. Centralized stores of data are a surveillance state's dream;

all of your citizens' data in one easily accessible place and the ability to monitor it without their knowledge. Amazon Web Services, Google Drive, Dropbox, and every other "cloud" provider, despite having a distributed computing backend, are centrally owned.

Additionally, as the global economy rapidly evolves from a labor-based economy to an information-based economy, with robotics and automation technology expanding at an accelerating rate, data will become the primary form of value. Although humans can't compete with robots for labor, they can compete with them for data, the data they parse from their unique perception of the world, the processed output from their five senses. We not only possess our data, we need to own our data as the world evolves.

So how do we solve this? How do we store data in a decentralized way such that no one but yourself owns your data? This is a problem that has been under heavy research for at least a decade with several parties claiming a solution. The ideal solution should provide a method of storing data in a decentralized way that is robust and as trustless as possible.

Option 1: Storing Data Directly in the Bitcoin Blockchain

This is the naïve method. Yes, it solves the decentralization of data because everyone who has a copy of the blockchain is storing it, but no one can alter it. The data can, of course, be encrypted by using SHA-256 so that everyone who has a wallet will store a copy of your data, but only you would be able to access it given that you have the private key. But the Bitcoin blockchain was not meant to handle massive amounts of data! Its design purpose—which it serves well—is storing simple transactional logs. Even with only this burden, the blockchain has grown to 38 GB over the past couple of years. Downloading the blockchain can take up to several days, and scalability and blockchain bloat have consistently been serious concerns among the core developers. When you upload data to the blockchain, you are forcing Bitcoin miners to store your data for free, removing the incentives for them to maintain the network because the cost margin to participate is higher than they are getting paid.

What about storing data in a different blockchain with increased size limits to allow for extra data? Assuming miners were paid for storing your data with your altcoin, even then the blockchain's size would grow to insane limits and everyone who wanted to actually use your altcoin would need to download an unnecessarily massive wallet. This already looks ugly if you imagine many users storing even a few images, but we are moving toward a new era of data distribution in which petabyte datasets will soon become common. Storing data on the blockchain is not a short-term solution to achieving a robust decentralized data store, and it most definitely is not a long-term solution.

Option 2: Storing Data in a Distributed Hash Table

Distributed Hash Tables (DHTs) have taken off in popularity in the past decade. They distribute not only copies of the data, but also the indexing functions that enable the data to be found, ensuring resiliency. Early peer-to-peer (P2P) filesharing programs like KaZaA, Napster, and Gnutella used their own versions of DHTs with varying levels of decentralization. Some had centralized trackers to monitor the movement of all data and some (like Napster) had central sources that all data had to go through, leaving them with a single point of failure (in this case, due to legal action).

The first implementation of a DHT to really take off was BitTorrent. BitTorrent is still used by more than 300 million users. Despite having a decentralized data store (the BitTorrent Mainline DHT), it still depends on centralized trackers (like Pirate Bay) to monitor the network. Sites like Pirate Bay are regularly shut down by legal action, so even with BitTorrent's data resiliency, it still has some points of failure. If we use BitTorrent's DHT to store our dapp's data, that would be great, right? BitTorrent doesn't just offer a decentralized data store; it offers a data distribution protocol that maximizes bandwidth via a tit-for-tat strategy between seeders and leechers.

BitTorrent's data transfer protocol is even faster than the Web's, and as such it's become the de facto method of transferring large datasets like HD movies over the Web. The problem with using BitTorrent as a data store is that there is not enough incentive to store your data for the long term among nodes. The network is set up to prioritize files with high demand—people have to want your data for it to be replicated and continually stored in the network. In contrast, when using a reputable central server like Amazon Web Services, you know that your data is going to continue to exist even if you are the only user of the data, because their reputation is at stake, they are contractually obligated to do so, and they don't depend on others needing the data to store it.

First, we don't just want the decentralized storage capabilities of a DHT and the speed of BitTorrent's file transfer, we also want data permanence. It's necessary, therefore, to incentivize nodes to store data in some way. Second, we need to ensure that the links to the data don't die. This is not a new idea. One of the original proposals for the Internet had link permanence baked in. That idea was called Project Xanadu, and it called for a Web in which every link worked two ways: one toward the destination, and one toward its source. That means that the content creator would always be able to get credit for their data because it would always link back to them. This Web never came to be, and so we have the HTTP-based Web we've grown to know and love today with one-way links.

But does there exist a system that implements these features? Yes, it's called the Interplanetary File System (*http://ipfs.io*) (IPFS), and it's an open source project that is currently in alpha phase. I'm a pretty big fan of IPFS and was one of the early contributors to the protocol. Juan Benet, the creator, had been thinking about data storage for five years and had finally put all those thoughts into action when he published the IPFS scientific paper (*http://bit.ly/ipfs-whitepaper*). I spent many months understanding the system and his frame of thought, why IPFS was better than other solutions being worked on, and at this point I feel it has the best chance of bringing the most value.

IPFS aims to help us move toward a permanent, decentralized Web. That is, a Web whose links never die and no single entity controls your data. Upon downloading an IPFS client, a user is able to add any data to it and in return receives a hash. The user can then access that data via its hash. IPFS is a content-addressed system, in contrast to the Web, which is an IP-addressed system. In an IP-addressed system, if a name-server fails, effectively so does all of its data. Content addressing is a much more efficient form of addressing data because it doesn't rely on a single server's uptime to access data. When you request data from a content address, you'll receive it faster than you would IP-addressed data because it will route from whoever owns a copy of that content address closest to you.

So, what does it look like on the backend?

IPFS uses a DHT to store data. It's based on the popular Kademlia DHT, and it borrows ideas from Chord and BitTorrent's DHT. When users upload data to IPFS, that data is copied among a certain number of other nodes, so even if one node fails, the data remains. On top of that—and like BitTorrent—the more nodes that need the data, the more resilient it becomes as they each share the copy they download. Chord's killer feature was its DHT circles, which created "chords" to maximize DHT lookups among nodes across the globe that were in close proximity to one another within larger chords. So, the globe would look like a series of increasingly larger chords (see Figure 2-1) and lookups would benefit from this efficiency, hopping between chords where necessary.

Currently, centralized services like Amazon and Google have datacenters across the world that a user can choose from—in many cases they will automatically choose it for you—through which to receive and route your data. Even with datacenters spread across the globe, data transfer efficiency can be increased with multiple nodes in a way only a truly decentralized system like Chord's DHT can provide.

To give structure to the DHT and let users find the data they need when they need it, IPFS uses what it calls a *merkleDAG*. A merkleDAG is a simple flexible data structure that can be conceptualized as a series of nodes connected to each other. To be more specific, it's a directed, acyclic graph (DAG). A merkleDAG can look like a linked list or a tree. When adding data to the DHT, the system generates an SHA-256 multihash public-private key pair, and the user gets both. Developers can link hashes programmatically to form their own mini-merkleDAGs, and it's important to note that all data in IPFS forms the same generalized merkleDAG consisting of all nodes. All data on

IPFS is public, so it's the users' responsibility to encrypt their data accordingly. The private keys, in addition to allowing access to the data, can prove ownership.

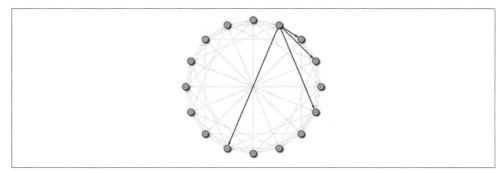

Figure 2-1. Chord

IPFS (shown in Figure 2-2) was inspired by BitTorrent's speed of transfer and tit-for-tat mechanism of finding nearby peers to share data with, and the IPFS team believes the Web should work that way, as well. Take the example of an entire college class requesting a video from a centralized Facebook server. This takes up unnecessary bandwidth and is unnecessarily redundant. If the image is nearby, they don't need to make a request from that far away. In a content-addressed system, if they know the content address of the data they want, they can just retrieve it from the nearest location. Nodes can share data among themselves without central coordination; the schema takes the server-client model that the HTTP web runs on and makes it distributed, just like BitTorrent.

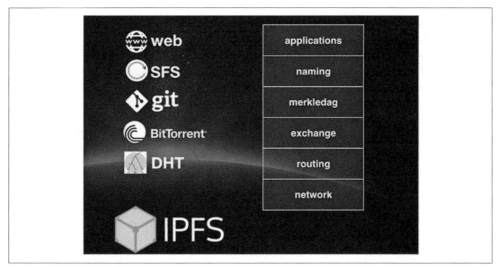

Figure 2-2. IPFS

How Does IPFS Improve on BitTorrent?

IPFS has a sister protocol called Filecoin (*http://filecoin.io/filecoin.pdf*). Filecoin is used to pay miners (nodes that store data) using a novel value-for-data mechanism called BitSwap. Cryptocurrency makes sense here: its value transfer is fast and it allows for micropayments to pay for every correlated byte of storage. Filecoin is currently in development, but IPFS is already available to use. IPFS commands are currently free and the miners currently storing data are doing so out of their love of the network. Eventually, all uploads and downloads will require Filecoin. Filecoin will most likely be an asset built directly on Bitcoin's blockchain, so users can just use their Bitcoin to pay for storage.

To top it all off, IPFS borrows from Git's version-control model to version all data. Git uses a DAG to model versions of data and IPFS uses it to give structure to the entire system. Users can see the version history of their data (or any data to which they have decrypted access).

So, IPFS takes the best ideas from Git, DHTs, SFS, BitTorrent, and Bitcoin and combines them to create a decentralized data-storage network. IPFS hopes to one day replace the HTTP:// protocol of the Web with IPFS://, but they can work in unison as well in several ways that we'll get into when we begin talking about implementation.

IPFS is the most robust, thought-through solution to decentralized storage out of all the cryptocurrency projects, although there are other notable contenders in the space, as well. Let's survey the other options.

Ethereum Swarm
> Ethereum (*https://ethereum.org*) is working to build a general-purpose (Turing-complete) blockchain computing language, including decentralized storage. As of this writing (2016), their efforts are focused on securing the DAO (in their usage, "Democratic Autonomous Organization") and storage has been put on the back burner.

StorJ
> StorJ (*https://storj.io*) has garnered a lot of hype lately; it has pre-mined a lot of StorJcoins and has made some pretty designs. The designs are neat—it won an Austin hackathon—and the group seems to know what it's talking about. Despite all of this, more than a year post-hackathon it is still vaporware.

Maidsafe
> Maidsafe (*https://github.com/maidsafe/Whitepapers/blob/master/Project-Safe.md*), like Ethereum, is trying to do many things. They aren't using proof-of-work and aim to create a decentralized platform for computing, storage, and currency. They've been working on their platform for six years and it seems like the project hasn't gained that much traction.

Decentralized Wealth

Bitcoin was the first successful decentralized store of wealth. Before Bitcoin, trust was needed in a third-party provider (a bank) when transferring value over the Web. Bitcoin allowed for decentralized value transfer and fulfills the need for decentralized payments in a dapp.

But what about all of these altcoins? And what about Litecoin, dogecoin, peercoin, darkcoin, and kanyecoin? Altcoins are generally made by forking the Bitcoin source code and adding in an incremental feature that for a variety of reasons the core developers of Bitcoin have refused to adopt. For example, the Litecoin (*https://litecoin.com*) creator wanted faster payments than Bitcoin so he forked Bitcoin, added some speedy code, and Litecoin was born.

Litecoin has a pretty big market cap, having been consistently in the top five cryptocurrencies for at least a year. Litecoin is a rare example that serves a good purpose: faster payments. But most altcoins don't: if they're not jokes that become memes with money behind them (like dogecoin), they are just made for "pump-and-dump" schemes. The idea is that someone can just create a new coin, slap a label on it, and pump up its value by hyping it via media exposure (kanyecoin). They claim that a coin will be really valuable and that investors will make a lot of money by buying in early as the coins value goes up.

As soon as the coin appears to have enough value, the creators sell it all for a currency that is more stable and long-term like Bitcoin or fiat. This is a common scheme in the altcoin world, and it is terrible for the cryptocurrency ecosystem for obvious reasons. First of all, these coins tarnish the reputation of cryptocurrency in general because they make potential investors increasingly wary of the space. Second, they compete with the Bitcoin blockchain for market share unnecessarily while bringing no real value to the table. This in turn harms Bitcoin's value and all of those that rely on it as the most-used cryptocurrency.

Bitcoin, of course, uses the proof-of-work scheme, which means that every miner in the network must generate a computational proof of their computing power and process transactions; in return miners get Bitcoins as payment for their maintenance of the network. Some people in the cryptocurrency space consider proof-of-work to be overly energy expensive and a short-term solution to Sybil resistance, so a whole host of cryptocurrency research is ongoing in the field of consensus mechanisms. Proof-of-work uses a lot of computing power and the total cost of the electricity spent by miners in maintaining the network is more than 15 million dollars. This is wasteful when there potentially could be better ways of maintaining the network. Two popular alternatives that have been proposed to replace proof-of-work are proof-of-stake and delegated proof-of-stake.

Despite the massive amount of ongoing research into novel consensus mechanisms post Bitcoin, like proof-of-stake, nothing has currently shown itself to be as Sybil-resistant as the proof-of-work. As computationally expensive as it is, it's the best we have. The Bitcoin network has more than three billion dollars invested in it, and countless startups, investors, media, and retailers accept the currency. It has the first-mover advantage and has fought for five-plus years to gain recognition among the mainstream populace. We shouldn't need to start over again. Even if a new consensus mechanism is found that is superior to proof-of-work, we should rely on the Bitcoin core developers to implement it rather than an altcoin so that we can progress faster as a community.

Some may call this idea "Bitcoin Maximalism." The argument is that Bitcoin maximalists continually tout the first-mover advantage of Bitcoin and are staunchly against any competitor to protect their investment in the network. The negative implication of Bitcoin Maximalism is that any ideas outside the Bitcoin protocol, no matter how valuable, are quickly stamped out and not given their proper recognition by the community, and progress is put on hold.

There is a solution that gives us the best of both worlds: this is called the *sidechain proposal*. The sidechain proposal is based on a paper (*http://bit.ly/back-sidechain*) coauthored by Adam Back, the inventor of proof-of-work that Satoshi referenced in his Bitcoin Paper (*https://bitcoin.org/bitcoin.pdf*). This proposal starts from the idea that in order to experiment with consensus mechanisms and any novel cryptocurrency ideas currently, developers must fork the Bitcoin blockchain and create an entire new altchain to test out their hypothesis.

This is bad for Bitcoin, and it's difficult for developers to bootstrap a blockchain. The solution proposed by Back's team is code that effectively allows Bitcoins to move freely between the main chain (the Bitcoin blockchain) and sidechains. That means that you could create an entirely new blockchain and sidechain it to the Bitcoin blockchain easily. You would gain the security benefit of Bitcoin's proof-of-work, so you wouldn't need to bootstrap your own mining network. You would also get people already invested in the cryptocurrency experiment (people who own Bitcoin) as a base of potential users in your chain because they could just use the coins they already have. Lastly, you could send coins between the two chains without any conversion necessary. Two-way sidechains are currently in the works and will be released very soon.

The Bitcoin blockchain is the most secure blockchain; it has more computing power than all the world's supercomputers combined, so it's the most Sybil-resistant. Bootstrapping a proof-of-work blockchain from scratch is difficult; because computing resources are so small in the early stages, it's easy for an attacker to build up 51 percent of the total computing power of the network and take it over. Besides that, developers shouldn't need to worry about bootstrapping a blockchain in addition to the already challenging task of building a decentralized application that people want. Sidechains offer a solution here if you want to experiment with consensus mechanisms or implement some novel cryptocurrency technique.

But what about if you don't really want to implement a new cryptocurrency technique and just want to issue your own internal currency for decentralized application? A currency that grows in value with the network, allows users to access scarce resources, and incentivizes them to grow the network? Then there is no need to create a new (side)chain. You can simply create an asset directly on Bitcoin itself. Colored coins is my project of choice on the matter, though as usual there are a few notable alternatives:

Counterparty

Counterparty (*https://counterparty.io*) is a Bitcoin 2.0 protocol that lets users create and manage assets, enact bids, and place bids, and even allows for users to create Turing-complete contracts on top of Bitcoin. This all sounds awesome, but the problem is that Counterparty baked all of these interesting features into the protocol instead of modularizing them and layering them on top of each other. Issuing assets on the Bitcoin blockchain and letting users transfer them with the ease of Bitcoin is an awesome idea. But they've combined that with the dividend function. Distributing dividends is a nice little feature to have, but they are their own internal operation within Counterparty, instead of using native Bitcoin to track assets. Everything has been forced into the same overwrought protocol.

Bets are an example of adding an experimental and challenging feature with a good one: assets. What would be better would be to build simple layers, each really good at doing one thing. Modularity is the hallmark of good software, and Counterparty, as ambitious as it is, is not modular at all. If we envision a market of libraries of different protocols, those libraries will compete with one another, and the ones that are best will win. Imagine if all those useful libraries were hopelessly intertwined as one package. You would need to install all of them or none of them at all. That would be a nightmare, and that's exactly what Counterparty has you do.

Counterparty introduces an unwanted and confusing element to the developer who plans to use it: the XCP currency. If you want to build an appcoin using Counterparty's API, you will need to deal with XCP and all the conversions that go along with it. If you want to create any kind of asset, according to the protocol you must destroy 0.5 XCP—greater than a dollar at current prices. The XCP monetary supply is fixed, and because the currency is continuously destroyed every time someone issues a new asset, the entire monetary base is constantly in decline.

The fact that XCP even exists and is required to use certain features of Counterparty is an annoyance to developers. It means that you have to continuously look at the ticker price (XCP/BTC) to use it. There are entire platforms that exist to track this price, with real-time bidding and asking for liquidity, just like in any market. But really, what's the point? Why should you be forced to deal with all of that when all you want to do is create an internal currency for your app? It's basically a huge barrier to entry that no one really needs and, as such, it's a bad idea.

Counterparty updates its clients all the time, and people that depend on its API, like the Gems (*http://getgems.org*) app, get mixed results because of this. Because there is no modularity, if there is a bug, everything will break and has broken all at once. All in all, Counterparty is too centrally administered; there are better alternatives (colored coins) that provide the necessary modularity and decentralization without the additional currency to use.

Hyperledger

Hyperledger (*https://www.hyperledger.org*) believes itself to be "token agnostic," in that it allows an issuer to issue coins that are based on no underlying currency: neither Bitcoin, nor fiat, nor any other altcoin. The principle behind this is sound, but in practice it isn't because it relies on an unknown consensus mechanism that it touts is in the works. We've seen a lot of research in this field, and again nothing has demonstrated itself to be as versatile as proof-of-work.

One way to easily cut through the noise of any Blockchain 2.0 projects claims is to dig into their consensus mechanism. If it doesn't use proof-of-work or isn't based on Bitcoin, see how big their market cap is and dig into how many times there have been security breaches. Every time I've done this I've found security breaches. Table 2-1, from Meher Roy, summarizes the different beliefs in this field.

Table 2-1. Political cryptocurrency beliefs

Belief/bet	Platform opportunities	Incremental risk	Advantages
Level I	Not applicable	Not applicable	Not applicable
Token agnosticism	Hyperledger, Eris, Codius, Ripple/ Stellar	Lack of solutions for Identity and Private Key management Regulatory uncertainty resulting from end users controlling transactions Platform-specific flaws like weak consensus algorithm	Applicable to all assets including flat money, shares, and cryptocurrencies Can replicate all applications pioneered by cryptocurrency community Relative compatibility with existing regulations

Belief/bet	Platform opportunities	Incremental risk	Advantages
Cryptocurrency maximalism	Bitcoin, Ethereum, Tendermint, Pebble, Ripple/Stellar (partially), etc.	Societal inertia to new forms of value, needs massive network effect System that possesses sound monetary policy and consensus method, fast transaction speed, and is scalable appears late Associated political ideologies prevent mainstream growth	Market segment dissatisfied with conventional banking system is a ready market Significant public interest for the time being
Bitcoin maximalism	Sidechains	New technologies that improve on network maintenance cost, transaction speed, and scalability outcompete Bitcoin	Significant first mover advantage for Bitcoin
Hyperbitcoinization	Not applicable	Opinion proves to be a delusion	None

Token agnosticism is a strong set of views, but I believe Bitcoin can cooperate with existing financial systems. We've grown past the initial honeymoon phase of Bitcoin, during which many thought it would dominate the global currency landscape, and we've also realized that the banking system does have its place in the world despite how antiquated it is.

What about Turing-complete smart contracts? This is the second part of a financial instrument necessary for creating a decentralized payments system in a dapp. The Ethereum team has probably made the most progress on this, but it has big ambitions. Ethereum wants to create a Turing-complete blockchain, a decentralized storage network, a decentralized communications protocol, a new consensus mechanism and a new (bootstrapped) blockchain, a new browser in which to run Ethereum dapps, and a new scripting language with which to code Ethereum dapps.

Let's step back for a second. One team cannot and should not aim to accomplish all of these company-sized ideas single-handedly. Ethereum has raised a lot of money and a lot of hype, but despite Vitalik Buterin's brilliance, I don't think we should expect them to create the next Bitcoin. As Gavin Andresen, head developer of the Bitcoin protocol, said, they're either going to be playing security whack-a-mole or will scale down their blockchain massively.

The idea of a Turing-complete scripting language is useful; it allows you to do everything and anything that you want. Bitcoin's scripting language is purposely limited to prevent malformed (whether through malice or incompetence) scripts like infinite loops. Gavin Andresen said most of Ethereum's aims could be implemented in Bitcoin, and the core developers have already started implementing some of them.

For the sake of dapps and the scope of this book, we're only going to concern ourselves with asset creation and smart contracts; bets, derivatives, and protocols that require a separate currency are not things I will be discussing. Pragmatically, the simplest way to get people to use your dapp is to ensure that it is compatible with a currency they already own, and the largest one is Bitcoin. So, you should issue a colored coin either on top of Bitcoin or on top of a sidechain, which is essentially just Bitcoin underneath the hood with some additional features like faster transactions.

Decentralized Identity

The notion of identity has been debated for centuries, and in the Internet age, the term takes on a whole new meaning. What is identity? Who owns identity? How should identity look on the Internet?

Due to the recent advancements in cryptography, a lot of the solutions have been "assume a public-key infrastructure." Basically, assume that people would be willing to store a private key safely and identity will be decentralized. Only those with the keys would have access to it. BitAuth (*https://github.com/bitpay/bitauth*) is a good current example of this. BitAuth uses Bitcoin's existing technology to create a public-private key pair using secp256k1. It allows for passwordless authentication across web services. It gives you a system identification number (SIN) that is a hash of the public key. It uses signage to prevent man-in-the-middle (MITM) attacks, and a nonce to prevent replay attacks. Your private key is never revealed to the server and you can store it safely and securely. Identity is decentralized, so instead of having to trust a third party to store your identity, you can just store it yourself.

Other attempts to consolidate identity on the Internet have been made, with varying degrees of success. One of the most prominent attempts has been the OpenID (*https://openid.net*) protocol. OpenID is a decentralized identity protocol that takes advantage of existing web protocols like HTTP, SSL, and URI. The idea is that identity is fragmented across the web already, and by using the OpenID protocol, users can transform existing URIs into an account which can be used at any OpenID-supported sites.

OpenID abstracts the need to store your identity with the service provider so that you can only use a trusted source and that your identity will be carried around the multiple providers. This attempt seems to be the most successful so far in consolidating identities: companies like Google, Yahoo!, and Twitter have been OpenID providers. This is good in a way: now we can carry our identity across different sites without having to reregister again and again. It's better not only because it's more convenient to not need to reenter details, but also because you don't have to trust novel services with storing your identity data. But OpenID still creates a potential security vulnerability because you are still trusting one of these service providers with your data.

The problem is also known as Zooko's triangle (see Figure 2-3), and Namecoin (*http://www.namecoin.info*) was developed to help solve it.

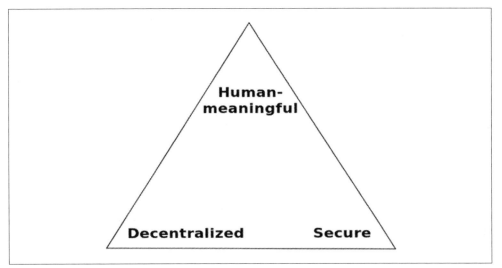

Figure 2-3. Zooko's triangle

Zooko's triangle is the conjecture that states that in a system that is meant to give names in a protocol, only two of the three desirable attributes (human-meaningful, decentralized, secure) can be achieved. OpenID solved security and human-meaningfulness. Namecoin completed it by adding decentralization to the mix. Namecoin was essentially a third-party identity provider, the blockchain itself, that you could use as an intermediary between you and the service requesting your identity. The Namecoin blockchain was one of the first forks of the Bitcoin blockchain, and it has stood the test of time because of the value it provides.

Whereas most altcoins wither away, Namecoin remains because no other innovation has completed Zooko's triangle. A user can "register" her name into the Namecoin blockchain by sending a transaction with her required name embedded in it under the */id* namespace. When the user sends the transaction, Namecoin stores it if it's unique—if no one has stored it before—otherwise it doesn't. That means the namespace is limited to the names people can think up. Although this means that users can create and select their own (human-legible) identities, it can create a new problem because of the limits of human-legible phrases. Fragmentation of identity does benefit the user because in a new service, you get a whole new namespace from which to choose identities.

In other words, this is a tradeoff: having a universal identity provider that completes Zooko's triangle is an important innovation, but the namespace is limited. Be that as it may, this is also the case with domain name registration. Currently ICANN controls name registration, a centralized organization backed by the United States Department of Commerce. (As of this writing, this is under tentative agreement to achieve formal independence in September 2016.) Namecoin has proved popular for registering *.bit* domains as a decentralized alternative to ICANN. These *.bit* domains can't be accessed from regular browsers like Chrome or Firefox. To access them, the user currently must use either a *.bit* web proxy or download an extension. As *.bit* grows in popularity, it is possible that the protocol will be adapted by the browser natively.

Most people won't need to create a *.bit* domain; it adds friction between you and your end users because they need to install extra software or go through a proxy to access your website. But if you have some message you need to get across, something your government or other authority figure doesn't want you saying, *.bit* plays a perfect role in freeing you from Internet censorship.

So registering a username in the Namecoin blockchain is relatively easy. You just exchange some Bitcoin for Namecoin, download the wallet, and register the name. But what about logging in to the Namecoin blockchain? How does authentication and authorization work? Recently, NameID (*https://nameid.org*) was created. It combined the best of both worlds; a user can use his Namecoin */id* to log in to all of the thousands of openID-enabled websites. This reduces the barrier to entry for Namecoin to enter the mainstream app market.

So what's the catch to decentralizing identity? Well, it's the same catch as there is in decentralizing data and wealth with IPFS and Bitcoin, respectively: the user must store his private key. This is fine for hackers, who love decentralization and privacy. They are the most ideological population when it comes to using the right tools on the Internet. Hackers pride themselves on their innate drive for efficiency and perfection in the tools that they use. They encrypt their communication with GPG and use Tor clients to safeguard their browsing history from nosy ISPs and governments.

Storing some extra private keys for the sake of decentralization is undoubtedly the right thing to do for them. What about the mainstream populace? Do they really care about these things? I don't think privacy and decentralization are on the top of their minds. Combine that with the average level of computer-security literacy, and I think it's fair to say that most people are probably not able or willing to securely store encryption keys. The market demand for centralized storage is evident in the success of Coinbase (*https://coinbase.com*), Bitcoin's largest application so far. Coinbase is the exact opposite of decentralized: it's a bank for Bitcoin. It provides private-key storage as a service.

A lot of the Bitcoin community is against any form of centralization; some eschew even the slight centralization in the forms of trackers in BitTorrent. The real question is this: How far are you willing to go to decentralize your software? Do you want to decentralize your domain name and make users store three separate sets of keys, as well? The answers to questions like this depend on who your audience is and if the benefits of decentralization are worth it. When it comes to something like "decentralized Dropbox," a competitor to the current Dropbox, the answer may well be yes. If a competitor could come along and promise decentralization of its data with the same security benefits, I'd wager that there are enough people who think that's a great reason to securely store a private key in order to make such a system work.

Even in cases for which those people don't want to, some sort of business will come up that offers Storage-as-a-Service. I have to admit, even as a longtime Bitcoin user myself, I use Coinbase's services to store my Bitcoins. I just don't want to have to worry about them getting hacked on my computer! I'm willing to trust Coinbase more because it holds so many users' assets, the CEO seems trustworthy to me (or at least much more so than Mark Karpelès of Mt Gox), and it is backed by a pair of trusted investors (Andreessen Horowitz and Union Square Ventures).

I don't think we should necessarily be out to create completely trustless systems, but instead more trustful systems. I like the example of a train. Imagine a train that is going from San Francisco to Los Angeles that suddenly crashes. If the train has centralized its control to the conductor, the world knows whom to hold accountable (the conductor). If control of the train was completely decentralized to every passenger, no one could be personally held accountable so it would be difficult to find the bad actor.

Decentralization is not good for its own sake; it must have purpose and a real use case. Dapps can range in the level of decentralization they go for, and their levels will depend on their individual use cases. When it comes to creating a protest-forming app in China, the dapp should be decentralized, top-down, no questions asked. If it's a social network for which your goal is wide acceptance, using .bit is probably not the best idea for a domain name.

So, if you're using a dapp that is storing data on IPFS and issues a native currency using colored coins on the Bitcoin blockchain, you'll probably also want to use NameID to store user identities. There will then be three sets of keys consolidated into some kind of either local or third-party key store that the user will employ to access and utilize your software.

Decentralized Computing

So, we've covered decentralizing identity, data, and wealth, but what about computing? Can you store your web app directly in IPFS and run it? Well, yes and no. IPFS is just a file system, and like any file system, you can easily run and display static websites on it perfectly fine from the browser. But when it comes to what we today call backend apps—dynamic apps, apps that require a shell and compiling environment to run, such as Node.js and Ruby on Rails—IPFS cannot do that. Thus, even if your app's data is stored on IPFS, where do you store the source code?

Well, there are two options. The first is to store the data in IPFS and host your source code on a traditional virtual machine (VM) for web apps like Heroku. A VM is an emulation of a particular computer system. VM operation is based on the computer functions and architecture of a hypothetical or real computer. VM implementations might involve specialized software, hardware, or some combination of both. Heroku is a popular Platform-as-a-Service (PaaS) offering that provides the capabilities of a VM easily to a user. It can run dynamic backend code like Go and Node.js, and also store your data with an internal hosting service utilizing databases like MongoDB.

If you store your source code on Heroku and your data on IPFS, users can trust that the data belongs to them and you aren't selling it to outside sources for profit. But what they can't do is trust that the source code you open-source is what's actually running on the server. Aside from this lack of verifiability, it also means that there is a central point of failure (Heroku). A second way to deploy is by storing your users' data on IPFS and deploying your source code to a decentralized VM built on top of IPFS. Does this exist? The closest project to achieving this is astralboot (*https:// github.com/ipfs/astralboot*). Basically, this is a golang server that pulls its files directly from IPFS and lets you run a Debian environment based on IPFS. This means that if you deploy a dynamic app on top of astralboot, it's built on IPFS and you need only configure your particular environment on top of astralboot's Linux environment.

There are other ideas like Ethereum's own EVM (Ethereum virtual machine). Ethereum's blockchain differs in many ways from the Bitcoin blockchain: different block times, Turing-complete contracts, and it acts as a decentralized-state machine because of it. I think it is a VM, but not a complete one and certainly not a VM that most developers would need. Requesting data from third-party sources is almost necessary in today's software market; there are a multitude of competing services that specialize in niche areas of data that offer their API to other services to you. Instead of having to reinvent the wheel every time and create trusted data sources for your app, you want to be able to use third-party APIs. The problem with Ethereum's EVM is that you can't get data from outside the blockchain unless it's been preconfigured to work with Ethereum by setting up a smart contract inside of its server.

This is great for new APIs that act as "oracles" (trusted federated sources of data), but it's not good for existing services. Neither the Ethereum blockchain nor the Bitcoin blockchain can request data from outside of itself. This is both an inconvenience and a security constraint purposefully implemented. If it were possible to call APIs from the blockchain, a hacker could outrun the blockchain with varying data requests, and eventually it would result in bloating the network. So using the blockchain alone as a complete VM is not a good idea.

Another project is Go-circuit (*http://gocircuit.github.io/circuit*), which creates small server processes that run instances on a machine cluster. They form a churn-resilient and efficient network, which enables distributed process orchestration and synchronization from any single machine. It's made for Go programs; it's a distributed run-time, and it has Docker integration. It's cool if your project is coded in Go, otherwise it doesn't work for you.

All this talk of decentralized computation begs the question: What if computing were a marketplace? Imagine a sidechain in which the proof-of-work did actual useful computation for the network—some coins like gridcoin (*https://gridcoin.us*) and primecoin (*https://primecoin.io*) already do this. But, they aren't utilizable (in a verifiable way) for new computations that users decide; they're based on existing computations that the coins' creators need. What is needed is P2P decentralized computing that allows for an easy-to-access interface to which dapp developers can deploy their code.

The network we desire would have its own compute coin, and dapp developers would pay miners, engines of computation, to compute their source code. As more users come on board, the value of the network—and subsequently the coins—would grow. This is an area of research for crypto, so as of now I believe something like astralboot, which is under heavy development, is our best hope to fastest method to prototype.

Even if astralboot is too difficult to configure, Heroku works just fine; if Heroku fails and your code is open source, anyone can just reupload it to a new server, accessing the permanent, user-owned, and publicly verifiable data living on IPFS. If the computation marketplace becomes possible, you'll be able to run dynamic apps directly from the browser as a domain on the web.

Decentralized Bandwidth

So far, we've talked about the four main points that can be decentralized in a dapp: identity, wealth, data, and computing. We've talked about domain registration, as well, which isn't as necessary for most use cases. To add to that list, let's discuss decentralized bandwidth.

For most users, ISPs act as gateways between you and the Internet (see Figure 2-4). There are several ISPs across nations that help connect people and act as the centralized hub; additionally they solve the "last mile" problem by connecting end users to the high-speed, high-capacity "trunk lines" of the Internet. The "last mile" is just a phrase used by telecommunication industries to refer to the last leg of the telecommunication network that delivers communication connectivity to retail customers. It's the Internet cable that actually reaches the customer directly.

ISPs like AT&T and Comcast are beneficial in that they give us Internet access where there is currently no other alternative. The downside is that these centralized gateways are also central points of failure. Governments can shut them down at will if they so desire. Governements can ask the ISPs to censor certain IP addresses that they don't want you accessing. ISPs will be forced to comply with the laws of the land and create a blacklist of web IPs that a user should not visit. There have been recent periods like the Hong Kong protests and the Arab Spring during which users feared government shutdown of ISPs. Some governments actually did shut down and censor Internet access by controlling these gateways maliciously to quell an uprising.

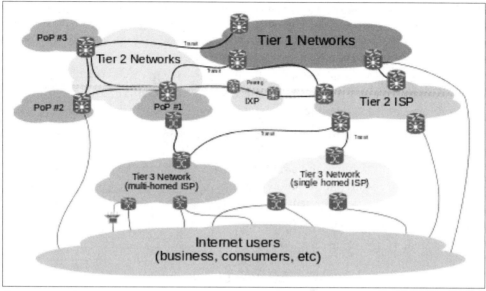

Figure 2-4. The Internet

It all works because there are no alternatives, but alternatives are beginning to appear. The latest example is the Firechat (*https://opengarden.com*) app for iOS, created by a company called Open Garden. Firechat lets phones speak to each other directly, peer to peer, using the iOS multipeer connectivity feature. No ISP is required. Firechat is an example of a *mesh networking* application. Mesh networks are the decentralized version of the standard centralized Internet. In a mesh network, users don't need to go through a central gateway to access a site; they can connect directly to the nearest router, which would be a nearby computer.

There are many *meshnets* already in use: Spain has one of the largest with more than 50,000 users who needed Internet access that no ISP provided. That meshnet is still in use. During a hurricane in New York, a meshnet was used to relay valuable rescue information when the lines were down. There are tons of meshes in San Francisco that are "dark" nets, as well, only open to visitors inside of the secret societies they instantiate. Meshnets don't generally have access to the regular Internet with all of its data. Without having tunneling in the loop, there is no access to the normal meshnet. Tunneling can only be done by switching from tunnel to mesh networking and back. Currently, doing both simultaneously isn't supported by any major hardware manufacturer, but you can have a hybrid and that is being worked on by projects like Open Garden and CJDNS (*https://github.com/cjdelisle/cjdns*). This one is a little harder than the rest because in addition to software changes, it requires hardware changes. Routers should have the ability to access both nets so that they can pull data from the regular Internet and use it on the meshnet so that it can't be shut down.

Although decentralized bandwidth is nice to have, it's only necessary in certain countries that censor Internet websites and block access to the Web altogether. I think that if this happens on a larger scale, a real need for this will cause decentralized bandwidth to become mainstream. Using the blockchain, we can have other computing devices act as gateways instead of ISPs. They could be paid for routing data using a cryptocurrency and proof-of-bandwidth.

Just as cryptocurrency enables P2P marketplaces for computing and data storage, it can enable it for bandwidth sharing. Cryptocurrency enables marketplaces where centralized power structures once existed. These could be marketplaces for computing, storage, bandwidth, and any of a wide variety of scarce resources both "real" and "artificial" that people can think up. We're going to see the economy shift more and more toward one based on information, and the market for data will more than likely be the biggest in the world as automation slowly eats away at everything labor based.

Decentralized Markets for Decentralized Assets

With marketplaces come financial instruments like derivatives, assets, currencies, and futures. A problem arises: Where can people exchange these assets? Traditionally we've used centralized stock exchanges to exchange assets, but how would this work in a decentralized information economy? Trading assets used to be decentralized before there was more infrastructure; for example, in barter economies. We can now combine the open exchange of information that the Internet provides with decentralized models of ownership verification and more. Goods can be thought of as assets in this case with no central oversight whatsoever. Governments have provided a trusted intermediary to ensure legitimate cross-border exchanges and value stability. A lot of trust goes into trading and securing assets; governments are the most trusted source we could create to pull this off so far.

Assets that are created by the government (like state currencies) have always been under the tight grip of government oversight. So, what happens when we add non-state-run actors into the mix? Currently, there are a lot of regulatory investigations into the Bitcoin network and how the United States government and other governments should regulate it. Bitcoin has been outright banned in some countries like Bangladesh. In some countries, Bitcoin is accepted by the government as legal tender and exchanges are able to occur with government oversight through existing stock exchanges.

For most countries, government opinion on Bitcoin is unsure at best—and suspicious at worst. Governments are still trying to understand this invention as it is only seven years old. They can be slow to change and the legal climate might prevent Bitcoin from ever entering their market. What is needed for an ungated, free, international market is a decentralized stock exchange for the new economy that doesn't depend on any central government or corporate entity monitoring it. In the information economy where dapps are mainstream, each user of a dapp is also consequently a shareholder.

The shares that they own are the native currencies of the dapps, colored coins, or Bitcoin sidechains in the most likely scenario. These currencies will fluctuate in valuation with the valuation of the dapp: as more people find the app useful, its valuation will grow, and so will its shares. Further, these shares can pay out dividends from the dapp's stream of revenue, making them even more valuable. Users will eventually want to trade these assets for more durable, stable forms of assets like currencies— maybe a USD-backed Bitcoin sidechain like bitUSD. BitUSD is a novel cryptocurrency pegged to USD that can be traded for BTC seamlessly. They could also trade for a price-stable cryptocurrency that has seignorage built in, or a currency with its own decentralized reserve. Users will needs stability in some of their assets, in short, and will eventually want to convert some coin to whatever will maintain their purchasing power when they are happy with their value and don't want to risk losing it from investment in a dapp.

So far, exchanges for cryptocurrency have relied on a centralized source to hold your money, so for the duration of the exchange you had to trust them. This has resulted in numerous thefts from—and, it seems, by—central entities, mostly because they are not backed by any governing legal contracts,given that Bitcoin is still under examination by most governments. The most infamous example is Mt Gox, an exchange based out of Tokyo run by Mark Karpelès. Gox was huge in Bitcoin's early days and a lot of people had used it. In February of 2014, it shut down, and there was no explanation as to the loss of customer funds. People were furious, but there was hardly a way to discipline Karpelès due to Bitcoin's murky legal situation.

Since then, people have grown more and more distrustful of exchanges. Ideally, we could list our dapp asset/stock prices on government stock exchanges, but that would take a lot of regulatory approval and people don't want to wait for that. On top of that, getting on a federal stock exchange requires a company to issue an IPO. An IPO requires a company to have a certain amount of capital in the millions, hire investment bankers and lawyers, and file mountains of paperwork. This is a very high barrier to entry and because the stock exchanges hold nation-based monopolies on trade, they are able to maintain that system.

Bitcoin has given us the opportunity—the choice—to opt out of the financial system and we should have that option. Not because the government is "evil" and "endlessly printing money," but because people should be given the option, and the more options the better. Let's decentralize the IPO and let early stage startups sell shares of their stock to people who aren't *accredited investors*. The accredited investor requirement limits the people who can fund a corporation to those with at least a million in the bank. Crowdfunding sites are useful, but they don't give funders equity in return because of this requirement. We need a decentralized stock exchange. So, how would it work?

There are some ideas that involve Ripple (*https://ripple.com*)-style mechanism of exchange. (Ripple-style meaning you can choose who to reach consensus with, as opposed to proof-of-work where you trust the majority of work). Stellar (*https://stellar.org*) is in some ways the new Ripple; its founder, Jed McCaleb, teamed up with some Stripe-backed teammates like David Mazieres (a brilliant Stanford researcher of distributed systems) and decided to create a new altchain. Stellar is quite literally the Ripple source code white-labeled with a new consensus mechanism that is still being ironed out.

The basic idea is that you can trade your currency with anyone else by trusting a third-party intermediary to administer the exchange. The trusted third party could be a bank or central exchange or even a friend. The system is interesting because unlike many altcoins, it's not completely decentralized. It adds in an element of interpersonal or organizational—that is, social—trust to facilitate exchange.

This isn't ideal, but truly decentralized order matching with zero trust hasn't been solved and is most likely impossible prior to a major leap forward in AI. Centralization has its downsides, but it also offers a positive: accountability. In the Stellar model, the intermediary nodes are held accountable for any mishaps, and if any occur, their reputation goes down. This model in and of itself has value, but the problem with Stellar, as with most altcoins, is that it introduces a new cryptocurrency and its consensus mechanism has yet to be proven to work.

Proof-of-work is the only known Sybil-resistant solution that works at scale. What does that leave us with? The most decentralized exchange I know is called Mercury (*http://mercuryex.com*) by a developer named Mappum. Mercury is a multicoin wallet that uses the *cross-atomic chain* (CAC) transfer protocol of Bitcoin to exchange value between cryptocurrencies. The CAC transfer protocol lets Alice and Bob, who own coins in separate cryptocurrencies, to exchange them without having to trust a third party. Both cryptocurrencies need to have the protocol implemented for it to work. The actual order matching is done on a server, but the wallet holds the values locally so there is no risk of theft. Mercury is an open source project that is available on GitHub and is actively under development but already has several users. As the wallet grows in popularity, users will want to store all of their assets in the wallet and exchange them with the click of a button for other forms of value. It's the predecessor to the holy grail of wallets, one that holds any and all cryptocurrency.

There likely won't be one that recognizes all the different competing protocols, just as web browsers don't recognize the Xanadu proposal or any of HTTP's other failed competitors as protocols. And yet browsers are used by everyone who wants to access the Web. Bitcoin, colored coins, and sidechains will win out in the end. BTC-blockchain-backed assets are the most secure due to the 500-plus supercomputer computation powered security of Bitcoin's blockchain, its first-mover advantage for market share and mind share, and its superb community of developers working to increase its scale. Any company can add its coin to the open-source Mercury wallet, no IPO necessary.

Even if Mercury doesn't win, the model is solid and it means the barrier to entry for IPO will be diminished for those who issue assets via cryptocurrency.

Practical Decentralization

Compliance with government regulations is a must for success in the modern world. One need only look at PayPal, and now Coinbase, to see how government compliance builds trust among users and lets a business grow internationally. Unfortunately, issuing assets for your registered corporation in the United States to people who aren't accredited investors on a decentralized stock exchange doesn't scream government compliance. So what can dapp developers do to create their dapps and move out of the shadows and into the mainstream alongside Facebook, Instagram, and Vine? Here are three suggestions:

- Start your corporation as a nonprofit
- In your legal documents, label your assets as app tokens to unlock features
- Add your asset listing to a decentralized exchange like Mercury

That's a solid beginning, and it might be all that's necessary with effective decentralization. You can offload the legal landmines of dealing with decentralized exchanges to the exchanges themselves. The exchange is decentralized, so it can't be shut down, except for the server that order-matches. But because the app is open source, users can either continually make new server backups or insert their addresses.

Using sidechains and colored coins eliminates the stress of having to deal with different chains that might or might not support CAC swap, which would require a patchwork of code to accommodate compatibility. If everything is just Bitcoin under the hood, life is easier for a programmer to build apps that use several different currencies. For example, imagine a decentralized Dropbox built on IPFS. Users would pay the underlying networks fee (Filecoin), possibly a fee to register their usernames on the Namecoin blockchain, and possibly some internal currency fee for the service. How does one transaction split up into three different currencies, hitting different chains? If everything is just Bitcoin under the hood, value can transfer seamlessly between the coins.

This is why Bitcoin seems the strongest basis to be the blockchain on which all other financial assets are built: it works better than anything else so far, it's simple to think about, and it's simple to implement. But what about having to decide between coins and their use cases? Bitcoin's transaction times could be faster. Litecoin as a sidechain can speed this up by a good amount. Then there's Darkcoin, which keeps your transaction history private by scrambling and encrypting the transaction data on the blockchain. Primecoin and Gridcoin let you utilize the proof-of-work to solve scientific problems rather than just have it go to waste as computational power to back the network. How can we cherry-pick the features we want out of different cryptocurrencies without having to hold all of them and pick and choose between them?

The answer lies in a universal wrapper for all cryptocurrency. Picture a wallet that stores all Bitcoin-backed cryptocurrency, similar to what Mercury aspires to be. This is useful, but still presents the user with having to worry about which currencies to spend and when. Instead of this, the user is presented with one currency balance and features that she can turn on and off at will. The wrapper would turn currencies into features that end users could easily switch between.

Installation on the backend could be as simple as Node.js's packet manager. Want faster transactions? `bpm install lite`. Private transactions? `bpm install dark`. Help compute scientific data? `bpm install solar`. Transactions would filter through the various blockchains necessary to ensure that they have all the features a user requests. Users could store assets separately, just as they do today in portfolio accounts/online wallets or in their currency wallet, as an all-in-one wealth management wallet.

Let's consider the practicalities: Storing currency in your computer wallet is dangerous. It's a decentralized alternative to banks and some people think it worth the risk because it's an ideological decision. Some people don't like the idea of banks—they can be corrupted, and given that they are central institutions they can fail; lots of people's eggs in one basket. But most people aren't ideological! It's the sad truth; most people don't care about centralization or data security or data ownership. They just want something that works well at solving their problems.

A bank solves a very important problem for people: secure storage of wealth. Storage as a service has been around for a very long time and continues to provide value to people. Coinbase, for example, is the most popular Bitcoin-based service and there's nothing decentralized about it. It has essentially become a bank: it not only holds your Bitcoins in a secure online wallet, it also has begun holding your USD, as well! As Coinbase becomes more popular, so does Bitcoin. It's very easy to use and takes the worry out of storage. If Bitcoin is ever going to become mainstream, banks will need to accept it as currency. It sounds radical, given that Satoshi created Bitcoin as a way to avoid the chargeback problem that all online transactions tend to have. Why would we store it in a bank? The distinction is akin to carrying dollars locally versus carrying them in your bankcard.

Bitcoin gives us the option to have chargeback-free transactions over the Web just like cash if we so choose. But most people will opt to use something like a bank. When a bank works well, it's a great service. We can spend our currency anywhere without worrying about it being stolen due to bank's insurance on our balance and with its security keeping us content. Traditional banks will either have to evolve to accept Bitcoin as a protocol for money transfer or be surpassed by new competitors like Coinbase. Imagine if your bank stored your Bitcoin balance, as well. It would show your balance in your native country's currency and it would have an associated account number, routing number, and Bitcoin public keypair.

If anyone sent you Bitcoin, it would go directly to your bank account. If anyone sent you state currency, it would go directly to your bank account. You would be able to turn on price stability as a feature due to the universal wrapper so your balance would be as stable as it is currently. You could spend your Bitcoin anywhere you spend state currency because they would become indistinguishable.

Bitcoin will find its niche. Most people don't care about the word Bitcoin and just want to use their own currency. The leaders in the Bitcoin space like Abra (*https:// goabra.com*) won't even mention the word Bitcoin. They will just use it as a protocol for fast reduced-fee international money transfer and micropayments.

Abra is a startup that aims to tackle the huge remittances market in the developing world by creating a series of decentralized tellers that will exchange state currency for Bitcoin, and vice versa. They use the term "digital money" instead of Bitcoin, a smart move that won't scare away mainstream consumers and will most likely boost their sales. As a very practical matter, outside of the Silicon Valley state of mind, people don't really care for Bitcoin.

The rise of Bitcoin ATMs is fascinating, but visit any developing country without proper financial infrastructure and you'll see the transition from an all-traditional ATM network to an exclusive all-Bitcoin ATM network isn't going to happen in our lifetime. Instead, Bitcoin should complement the existing payment infrastructure by making it faster and cheaper when needed (wire transfers, especially internationally), and allow for all the features that cryptocurrency can offer a user, like micropayments —which can in turn enable dapps like microblogging marketplaces.

No one will be forced to use a bank, an identity, data, or centralized computation, but they can make life easier. We have the choice to decentralize when necessary, and hopefully as users get more aware of the value of their data, the world will slowly began to understand the importance of securely storing public keys themselves.

## CHAPTER 3

Building Your First Dapp

Enough with the theory, let's get to building. I'm going to assume that you have built at least one software application before. Building a dapp isn't that much more difficult than building a regular app. The added complexity comes from having to think in a decentralized way and not having as many mature libraries at your disposal as a regular app developer does.

This chapter will take you through the process of building a decentralized Twitter clone from source. We'll cover the following:

- The Go language
- Decentralized architecture and the IPFS distributed data store
- Kerala, an IPFS interface
- Coinprism, a colored coins wallet service
- Mikro, a decentralized messaging app with an internal economy.

Go

We'll be using Go for our dapp. Go has garnered a lot of interest from backend developers for its simple callback-hell-free syntax, fast computational time, and concurrency friendly "go-routines." Erlang and Rust are two others that claim to be superior to Go, and perhaps they are in some ways, but unlike Go, their libraries are in a very, very early stage of development.

JavaScript is also pretty popular these days, and with the advent of Node.js, JavaScript developers are no longer limited to frontend roles. They can create and maintain the entire web stack with one language (and, of course, HTML/CSS). JavaScript is the language of the Web and JavaScript developers can use a wide variety of JavaScript frameworks to build their web apps. Although JavaScript is great, it has its weaknesses. Concurrency is nontrivial to implement and it has confusing value constructors. Go makes up for these and is built for more distributed-type systems.

I've developed web apps built by using Go and web apps built by using JavaScript. Both languages have their pros and cons, but I have to admit that I've found Go to be the most efficient for building dapps. Google created Go because it needed a language that could handle the Google-scale concurrent computation of large datasets as fast and efficiently as possible. Go was the answer to that problem, and its use internally at Google has increased significantly since its first release.

Go has the power and speedy compile time of C and the elegance and brevity of Ruby. It was built for distributed systems, and that's why I keep coming back to it when I think about building dapps. The fact that IPFS was built using Go is also a plus because you can integrate distributed file storage into your app without compatibility barriers. There are many Go-based web frameworks to choose from: Martini, Goji, Gorilla, and even Go's standard net/http package. I like keeping my dependency stack as lightweight as possible so I build with net/http, my go-to, and I only reach for other web app libraries as they become necessary.

Centralized Architecture

There are three paradigms that are commonplace when building a standard server-client–based web app. Let's discuss them a bit.

REST

The server-client model is relatively simple and has become the de facto way to exchange data across the Web. REST, or Representational State Transfer, is a set of guidelines and best practices for creating scalable web apps usually based on the server-client model. REST is a named practice (just like AJAX), not a technology in itself. It encourages use of capabilities that have long been inherent in the HTTP protocol, but seldom used. The user can just point his browser to the URL (Uniform Resource Locator) and by doing so he is sending an HTTP request. Each HTTP request has information in the form of parameters that the server can use to decide what kind of HTTP response to send back to the client who issued the request.

CRUD

CRUD stands for Create-Read-Update-Delete. These are the basic operations to be done in a data repository. You directly handle records or data objects; apart from these operations, the records are passive entities. Typically, it's just database tables and records. Whereas REST interacts with a working system, CRUD manipulates data in the system. Typically developers would use a database like MongoDB or MySQL to perform CRUD actions on their data.

MVC

MVC stands for Model-View-Controller, and it's currently the most popular software programming paradigm. Models manage core behaviors and data of the app. Views render the user interface for the app. Controllers receive user input and make the necessary calls to model objects and the view to perform certain actions.

Decentralized Architecture: Introduction to IPFS

So, what happens to CRUD and REST in a decentralized architecture? They become one and the same. This is because data will live in a decentralized network of computers owned by no one, as is the case with IPFS. Performing operations or handling requests on data locally is the same as doing it remotely. You and everyone else are the server and the client. This sounds more complicated than it actually is. IPFS is my decentralized storage solution of choice because it has gotten farther than any of the competitors in the space and synthesizes great ideas from years of research in the space with proven practices.

When you build your dapp, it won't run on a server; rather, it will run locally on all your users' computers. We still haven't solved decentralized computation, and uploading the compute to a centralized virtual machine (VM) like Heroku would defeat the purpose of decentralization, so the right way to deploy a dapp is as a downloadable binary. Users can download it to their desktops and then access the dapp using either a web browser or directly within a client interface—for example, Spotify or Skype.

Dapps will require data storage in some form or another and as such they will double as IPFS-distributed file storage nodes. An alternative would be to just use a third-party IPFS node on a server to store the data, but then that cloud provider would be a central point of failure. Inevitably someone is going to buy some Amazon EC2 space, host a node there, and offer IPFS-node-as-a-service to make it easier for beginners to get started with using it. The data would be replicated from there as people request files on a case-by-case basis. An IPFS cloud node would also be great for mobile dapps, given that running an IPFS node takes a good chunk of processing power, and that correlates to losing a good chunk of battery life for laptop users.

Nodes can be incentivized by uploaders to store data by being paid in dollars or a cryptocurrency. IPFS creator Juan Benet published a paper (*http://filecoin.io/filecoin.pdf*) for a currency called FileCoin to do just that, but work on it still hasn't begun and thus cannot benefit us yet. In the meantime, the floor is open for anyone to create incentive schemes for data storage alongside IPFS so that nodes don't need to be online to have their data available for use. The more decentralized, the better. Even if an IPFS node server was taken down, if the data were useful at all, there would be copies stored by everyone who requested it. Such is the beauty of IPFS and why the creator refers to it as the permanent web. You could potentially also pay the server to "pin" your data. Someone might not want your data now, but eventually they will. As long as *someone* wants your data, it will live on.

A mobile app would be cool to build, but for this demo tutorial I'm going to focus on writing a desktop dapp because IPFS still doesn't have a solid Swift/ObjC or Android wrapper.

Let's look at two key commands in IPFS:

ADD
> Add data to IPFS

CAT
> Read data from IPFS

Notice how there is no `delete` command. IPFS is the permanent Web! After you add data to the network, unless you are the only one hosting the data, there is no way for you to delete the data you've added. This is because other nodes will have a copy of the data as soon as they access it. Also notice how there is no `update` command, because IPFS has Git's methodology built in. When you update a file, the file itself isn't deleted, it's versioned. You can create a merkleDAG for that file such that the latest hash is the latest version of the file. All older versions still exist, and you can still access them if you desire.

When you add data to IPFS, you are essentially just broadcasting to the network that you have the data; you aren't actually sending it to someone's computer. That only happens when someone requests the data. And because the data lives on the network, manipulation is a result of commands to the network, as well.

IPNS (the naming layer on top of IPFS) gives the appearance that updating and deleting are possible through mutable names. With IPNS you can publish a DAG of data under your immutable peer ID, and then whenever someone resolves your peer ID, she can retrieve the DAG hash. IPNS can only store a single DAG entry per peerID, so if you want to update or delete data, you can just publish a new DAG to your peerID. We'll get into implementation details of this later in this chapter.

What about MVC architecture?

Well, it's still there. What? No wildly novel methodology for structuring my code? Nope, models stay the same, controllers use IPFS for data storage and retrieval, and views are just HTML/CSS/JavaScript.

What about smart contracts? What role do they play?

In a dapp, there are certain elements that need consensus via smart contracts that would usually require a server. Usernames are a great example, as are financial actions such as escrow and property ownership. Smart contracts are technically "models," and you can feed data into them via transactions, but they are not the de facto "model" in MVC architecture. They can work alongside your existing models but their utility really applies in specific scenarios. These will come up on a case-by-case basis, and we'll learn how to build smart contracts later on in the book. The saying goes that we need smart models, thin controllers, and dumb views.

Eris Industries has a framework for building dapps called the Decerver. It has a whole lot of literature on its website explaining how to use it and all of the different and revolutionary methodologies it is implementing to help make dapp creation easier. It says that the models are the smart contracts, but the problem is that smart contracts are pay-to-play and should be orthogonal to model creation. It's an unnecessary complexity. MVC still applies in a decentralized app and your controller will speak to blockchains and DHTs instead of servers.

What Are We Building?

For our first app, we're going to build a decentralized version of Twitter. The bitswap mechanism of IPFS would mean all the nearest nodes could just pull the data from the node hosting it locally. Decentralized Twitter would be a useful tool to have, but this isn't the first time it's been done. A Brazilian developer named Miguel Freitas created a Twitter dapp called Twister a few years ago. Alas, Twister was plagued by a variety of security bugs that spammers took hold of, and Freitas was forced to implement rough fixes using the only tools he had. The patches are rough because they employ techniques like making the new user complete a proof-of-work to verify her identity after signing up, which was done to prevent Sybil attacks. This creates a high barrier to entry for new users who just want to try the system without having to dedicate computing power to prove themselves a good actor. Twister is also relatively difficult to install and setup.

We can benefit from a new version of a Twitter dapp because we're going to utilize new technologies like IPFS and Bitcoin. We'll call the dapp Mikro, and it's a great first dapp to work on because it's like an MVP for dapps. The data is relatively simple and straightforward: you are a user and you output microposts. You can discover new users and see their microposts.

Setup

Let's set up our Go environment. I'm all about reducing complexity where it's not necessary. Luckily, Go has package installers for Linux (*http://bit.ly/go-pkg-linux*) and Mac OS X (*http://bit.ly/go-pkg-mac*). (Sorry, Windows users, we're going to focus on Unix-based systems).

The great thing about these package installers is that they will automatically install the Go distribution to *usr/local/go* and set our path variables. Path variables are one of those "gotchas" in software configuration. They link your libraries to Terminal keywords you can use to call them. If it didn't set our path variables, we would have to set them ourselves, like so:

```
export GOROOT=$HOME/go
export PATH=$PATH:$GOROOT/bin
```

In this example, $HOME is where we've installed Go (*usr/local/*).

After you've installed Go, let's test it to ensure that everything is working. In the *src/* folder, create a new folder called *tests/*, and inside that folder create a file called *hello-world.go*. Type in the following in Terminal to begin editing the file:

```
'nano helloworld.go'
```

Add the following code snippet to the file and save it:

```
package main
import "fmt"
func main()
{
fmt.Printf("hello, world\n")
}
```

Then, run it with the Go tool:

```
$ go run hello.go
```

If the console displays hello, world!, this means that Go has installed properly.

Great—now we want to install our dependencies. First and foremost, let's install IPFS. Go makes it relatively straightforward to install dependencies directly from its source on the Web. To install IPFS, type this into your console:

```
go get -d github.com/ipfs/go-ipfs
```

After installation, Source your bash:

```
Source ~/.bashrc
```

Dependencies that are installed via the go get command are fetched and built for you. They are stored in the *src* folder of your Go root folder. If you cd into your *src* folder, you'll find another folder called *github.com*. Go will slice the URLs that you pull libraries from such that each component of a URL becomes its own folder. So inside of the *github.com* folder, there will be a *jbenet* folder. Inside of that will be a *go-ipfs* folder, and so on. This is useful because if you pull a lot of dependencies from a single source, Go will automatically sort them for you in their respective folders. So all of your GitHub dependencies go in your *github* folder, with the names of the Git-Hub users you are forking from getting their own folder name.

To begin using IPFS, you need to initialize its config files on your system, as follows:

```
'ipfs init'
```

This will take a few seconds; it's adding bootstrapped (hardcoded) peers to your configuration and giving your node an identity key-pair to identify as a peer to the network when you add or pin a file.

When you type *ipfs* into your Terminal after init completes, you should get the following prompt:

```
ipfs - global p2p merkle-dag filesystem
ipfs [<flags>] <command> [<arg>] ...

  Basic commands:

  init      Initialize ipfs local configuration
  add <path>Add an object to ipfs
  cat <ref> Show ipfs object data
  ls <ref>     List links from an object

  Tool commands:

  config    Manage configuration
  update    Download and apply go-ipfs updates
  version   Show ipfs version information
  commands  List all available commands
  id            Show info about ipfs peers

  Advanced Commands:
  daemon    Start a long-running daemon process
  mount     Mount an ipfs read-only mountpoint
  serve     Serve an interface to ipfs
  diag      Print diagnostics

  Plumbing commands:
  block     Interact with raw blocks in the datastore     object    Interact
  with raw dag nodes  Use 'ipfs <command> --help' to learn more about each
  command.
```

These are all the commands in IPFS, and it means your installation was successful.

Now try to add something to IPFS:

```
ipfs add hello
```

It should return something that looks kind of like this:

```
# QmT78zSuBmuS4z925WZfrqQ1qHaJ56DQaTfyMUF7F8ff5o
```

This is the hash of the data you just added. That data still lives on your computer, but now there is a content address associated with it, and anyone who has that address can retrieve the file directly from your computer as long as you're online. As soon as he retrieves it, he will have the data as well. From there, people who want the data will pull it in bits from both your and their computer. The more peers who store the data, the faster the download will be, just like BitTorrent. Unlike BitTorrent, IPFS has the added benefits of versioning and a naming system built in.

Now that you've added some data to IPFS, let's try CATing it back:

```
ipfs cat <that hash>
```

This should pull and display hello in the console. It's pulling it directly from your computer.

The next dependency is Kerala. Kerala is a little wrapper I wrote around IPFS and Colored Coins to help us create decentralized Twitter, although it's general purpose so you can use it for other dapps as well. Kerala makes it easy for you to add data to IPFS to form a MerkleDAG. You can install it with the following command in Terminal:

```
go get -u github.com/llSourcell/go-kerala/kerala
```

Here's an example of how easy it is to add and retrieve data from IPFS:

```
//Start a node

node, err := kerala.StartNode()
if err != nil
{
panic(err)
}

//Add your text to IPFS (Creates MerkleDAG)

var userInput = r.Form["sometext"]
Key, err := kerala.AddString(node, userInput[0])

//Get all your text from IPFS (Retrieves MerkleDAG)

tweetArray, _ := kerala.GetStrings(node)
```

The first snippet of code starts a node, so your dapp doubles as an IPFS client. It starts up the daemon, so you broadcast yourself as a peer to the network. The second snippet of code lets you add text to IPFS. You can add any kind of data to IPFS: video, images, data structures. But for this example we are going to use the AddString method to simply add a string to IPFS. What the wrapper does is every time you add a string, it creates a new hash for that string. Then, it links that hash to the previous hash. The link is an abstract term but essentially what it means is if you request the hash of the latest string, it will also subsequently get the hashes of all linked strings.

The links from a data structure that IPFS labels as a MerkleDAG. It's a directed acyclic tree graph that you can use to relate data. This is a great use for a Twitter dapp; every time you tweet, the wrapper will just link it up with your previous hash and store that new hash locally in a text file on your computer called *output.html*. Only you know that hash's key and can access that data but you will be sharing it with other people on the network.

The last snippet of text essentially performs an "ipfs cat" on the hash associated with your peerID (using IPNS) and stores it in an array for you to use and display in your view.

You'll also use a lightweight dependency called `httprouter` that helps making web apps easier. You can install it by using the following commands in Terminal:

```
go get -u github.com/julienschmidt/httprouter
```

Now that you have all of our dependencies installed, you can go ahead and download the dapp we're going to be building from source. I've taken the liberty of writing the app beforehand—there is just too much code to ask you to write from scratch in one go—so it would be best if I walk you through the dapp in a detailed way after you download it, build it, and run it. In the console, type the following:

```
go get -u github.com/llSourcell/dapp
```

For your reference, these are all of the imports the dapp uses. All of them except for IPFS, Kerala, and `httprouter` are a part of the standard Go library:

```
import
        (
                "net/http"
                "github.com/julienschmidt/httprouter"
                "github.com/ipfs/go-ipfs/"
                "path"
                "html/template"
                "fmt"
                "log"
                "github.com/llSourcell/kerala"
        )
```

`cd` into the *dapp* folder in your Go workspace, and then, after running ' `go install .` '. In that directory, type ' `go run app.go` ' to run the app. Go to *localhost:8080* and you should see your profile page show up. It will look something like that shown in Figure 3-1.

There won't be any posts, because you haven't added any. (The graphic shows my profile page after I added a series of posts.) Now, submit four or five different tweets via the text field. After each submission, return to the home page and refresh to view them. The app consists of a home page that doubles as your profile page. It shows all of your posts. The app also has a discover page to help you find other users and their profiles. Let's call this demo app Mikro.

Figure 3-1. My screen

Routing

Let's take a look at the routes first. The app is using a generic thin lightweight routing library (httprouter) built on top of Go's native net/http package to make routing simple. Recall that in standard web apps the GET and POST methods are used frequently to relate page loads to data requests or sends. The same thing is happening in the routes, and the data actions (IPFS CAT and ADD) are happening alongside them.

In the main method of *app.go*, you'll find the routes:

```
//[2] Define routes

router := httprouter.New()
//Route 1 Home (profile)
router.GET("/", TextInput(node))

//Route 2 Discover page

router.GET("/discover", displayUsers(node))
//Route 3 Other user profiles
router.GET("/profile/:name", TextInput(node))
//Route 4 Add text to IPFS
router.POST("/textsubmitted", addTexttoIPFS(node))
//[3] link resources
router.ServeFiles("/resources/*filepath", http.Dir("resources"))
http.Handle("/resources/", http.StripPrefix("/resources/",
  http.FileServer(http.Dir("resources"))))
http.Handle("/", router)
```

```
//[4] Start server
fmt.Println("serving at 8080")
log.Fatal(http.ListenAndServe(":8080", router))
```

Start off by initializing the router as a struct:

```
router := httprouter.New()
```

As an aside, Go isn't exactly an object-oriented programming (OOP) language in the traditional sense like most other languages. It follows a model similar to OOP, but it is different. Structs are Go's version of Objects. Structs have fields and methods and they feel like objects. But in regular OOP, we use the `class` keyword to define objects. This helps with inheritance, but Go is designed without inheritance. Although this might seem like a bad feature at first, it's actually a pretty good thing. Inheritance can get messy when you have lots of classes and different interfaces and implementations extending each other down a hierarchy. Instead Go uses subtyping (`is-a`) and object composition (`has-a`) to define relationships between structs and interfaces.

Our first route defines the method we call when the user goes to the page *localhost: 8080/*. It's the page you first saw when you started up the app for the first time. `Route` 2 is the discover page. The discover page lets you see all peers on the network that are currently online and using the app. `Route 3` is a model URL. Notice the `:name` keyword after `/profile/`. It's used to load any user's profile; when you replace name with a user ID, the URL will load the profile model with the specified user's ID information. The user ID in this case would be the IPFS NodeID that's created when you start the IPFS daemon. Every IPFS node gets its own Node ID, and because your Mikro instance is an IPFS node, you will have one, too. `Route 4` adds text to IPFS as a `POST`. Whenever the user submits a post, it is added to IPFS via this route. `[3]` and `[4]` are configuration lines for linking the server to its resources and starting it up at port 8080 of *localhost*.

Data Storage and Retrieval

Notice the "start the node" code at the very top of the main method:

```
node, err := kerala.StartNode()
if err != nil {
    panic(err)
}
```

That's all it takes for your instance of the app to be a part of the IPFS network.

After you submitted your first five posts to the network, you saw each of them appear in the posts table underneath the "submit text" button, one by one. You just added your first data to the dapp! Remember, adding data to IPFS doesn't mean it's split into a million pieces and now lives on a bunch of different people's computers and no matter what happens, government or otherwise, no one can ever take it down. What you've done is broadcasted to the network that you own the data you've submitted. It's local, it's stored on your computer. If you go offline, so does the data.

This is the problem that some dapps like Twister had: You need to stay online at all times. But the great thing about IPFS is that it aims for permanence and makes it possible to reach a stage of data permanence. Whenever others in the Mikro dapp see your tweet, they will store a copy of it, as well. And this happens recursively throughout the network. The more people that CAT your data, the more places it's stored.

We're going to need that IPFS node struct throughout the app. All CRUD/REST actions are based on it. One option is to create a global var; it's certainly an easy way to start, but creating globals is bad practice, particularly because it makes debugging a nightmare at scale. Instead, we'll create a type and pass the variable into each method call in the routes:

```
type IPFSHandler struct {
node   *core.IpfsNode
}
```

We'll wrap the required router function with another function so that we can pass the node in as a variable. Let's look at the code that adds the data to the network:

```
func addTexttoIPFS(node *core.IpfsNode) httprouter.Handle
  {
return func(w http.ResponseWriter, r *http.Request, ps httprouter.Params)
{
r.ParseForm()
fmt.Println("input text is:", r.Form["sometext"])
var userInput = r.Form["sometext"]
Key, err := kerala.AddString(node, userInput[0])
if err != nil {
panic(err)
}

}
  }
```

We start off by parsing the form to get the input text as a string, and then add it to the IPFS network using the Kerala library's AddString method, with the node as one parameter, and the string as the other. We're going to get a key back as a return parameter. We then print it out. The key is the hash of the data we just submitted. And that's it; that's how you add data to the network. Now, let's see how you can read and display data from the network onto your profile page.

When you first start the app, it goes to the home directory at "/" and the TextInput(node) method is called. Like the previous function, we wrap it in a proper http method so that we can also pass in the node as a variable:

```
func TextInput(node *core.IpfsNode) httprouter.Handle {
    return func(w http.ResponseWriter, r *http.Request, ps httprouter.Params) {
```

Next, let's parse the URL to see if it has a nodeID (that is, peerID) in it. This method is the same method for other user profiles and your profile. We want to differentiate what we will do based on whether there is a userID in the URL:

```
var userID = ps.ByName("name")
```

This will tell us if there is a name. If there isn't a name (that means it's your home profile), Kerala will pull the merkleDAG hash from our own nodeID using the IPNS resolving strategy. If there is a name, Kerala will get the DAG associated with the name by resolving it. The DAG is an acyclic directed graph, so every time a hash is added to it, it points backward in time to all previous hashes. Does that mean a user's identity is constantly changing? No—that's what's great about IPNS. Kerala utilizes both IPNS and IPFS to work seamlessly together. It will associate the HEAD node of a particular DAG with a particular peerID, republishing to IPNS as necessary when new data is added.

We have two possible cases here that are codified. The first case is if the URL doesn't contain a peerID. This means that it's the home page, and we should be pulling your tweets:

```
if userID == "" {
pointsTo, err := kerala.GetDAG(node, node.Identity.Pretty())
tweetArray, err := kerala.GetStrings(node, "")
if err != nil {
panic(err)
}
```

In this case, we resolve your DAG hash from your peerID. Then, we CAT all your tweets from that hash.

If the tweet array is nil, we'll just nil to the frontend:

```
if tweetArray == nil {
fmt.Println("tweetarray is nil")
demoheader := DemoPage{"Decentralized Twitter", "SR", nil, true, balance }
```

If we have tweets, we'll go ahead and send those to the frontend:

```
else {
fmt.Println("tweetarray is not nil")
 demoheader := DemoPage{"Decentralized Twitter", "SR", tweetArray, true, balance}
```

The other case is if the URL does contain a peerID. This means that we're trying to view someone else's profile.

We'll go ahead and attempt to resolve that person's peerID:

```
pointsTo, err := kerala.GetDAG(node, userID)
```

If it resolves, we do exactly what we did before, extract tweets from the DAG and send them to the frontend. If it doesn't resolve, that means the user hasn't published any tweets to Mikro, so we'll just return nil, and a blank profile page will show up.

Passing and Displaying Data to the Frontend

Let's take a look at the template model we have for our profile at *index.html*.

We start out with reference calls to Twitter Bootstrap and jQuery, two popular frameworks for building simple web apps quickly:

```
<link rel="stylesheet"
href="http://maxcdn.bootstrapcdn.com/bootstrap/3.2.0/css/bootstrap.min.css">

<scriptsrc="https://ajax.googleapis.com/ajax/libs/jquery/1.11.1/jquery.min.js">
  </script>
<script
src="http://maxcdn.bootstrapcdn.com/bootstrap/3.2.0/js/bootstrap.min.js">
</script>
```

After we have imported our dependencies, we add in a navbar. After adding in our navbar, we add in our two main `div`s: the submit `div` and the post table `div`:

```
<center>
<div id="submitform">
<form action="/textsubmitted" method="post">
 <input type="text" name="sometext">
 <input type="submit" value="submittext">
 </form>
</div>
</center>

<br>
<div id="posts">
 <form name="tableForm">
        <body onload="insertTable();">
    <div id="wrapper" align="center"></div>
 </form>
</div>
```

Our submit `div` creates a standard text input and submits it by referencing the `/text submitted` URL via `POST` method. After a user clicks the submit input button, it will go to the URL with the string as a parameter and it will call the method we discussed earlier, `addTexttoIPFS`.

We're going to put our posts in an HTML table to keep them organized. Because posts are dynamically added, our table must be dynamically sized and resized with each new post. We'll use JavaScript to achieve this:

```
function insertTable(
{
    var arr = [
            {{range .Tweet}}
                {{.}},
            {{end}}
        ];
```

```
        console.log(arr.length);
var num_cols = 1;
var width = 100;
    var alignright = "<td style='text-align: right'>"
var theader = "<table id='table1' width = ' "+ width +"% '>";
var tbody = "";
for(var j = 0; j < num_cols; j++)
{
   theader += "<th text-align='left'><font face='verdana'>My Posts" +
     " </font></th>";
}
    var str1 = "{{ index .Tweet 1}}";
for(var i = 0; i < arr.length; i++)
{
    tbody += "<tr>";
       tbody += "<td>";
       tbody += "<b>" + arr[i] + "</b>";
       tbody += "</td>";
    tbody += "</tr>";
    }
var tfooter = "</table>";
    var endalignright = "</td>"
document.getElementById('wrapper').innerHTML = alignright + theader + tbody
   + tfooter + endalignright ;


}
```

We use the {{ }} brackets to reference the data (tweets) we passed in from the fron-tend via the Demoheader struct:

```
var arr = [
         {{range .Tweet}}
            {{.}},
         {{end}}
      ];
```

We then get the size of that array through JavaScript's native len method. We use that size as the upper bound of our for-loop and iterate through the array. Before the array iteration loop, we go ahead and create HTML headers for the table that are static. Next, for each element in the array we're going to create a new table object. Inside of each table row is going to be a post. Then, we end it by combing the static elements with the dynamically created elements in the loop with the line:

```
document.getElementById('wrapper').innerHTML = alignright + theader + tbody
   + tfooter + endalignright ;
```

At the bottom of the fill inside of the style tags, you'll find some of the styling I've added. Notice how it's completely plain because this is just a demo to get you up to the basics of creating a dapp, not Design 101.

Let's move on to the discover page. The home page lets you see your own tweets, and the *profile/:name* URL lets you see the home page of every user on the network. How do we find these users? With the discover page, of course! Most social apps have some sort of discover page, and Mikro is no different. When you click the discover button on the navbar, you will see a list of peers that looks something like this:

```
All peers
QmW3ssBgGLANKNKXiRxcQMmxg3FPd3tSwu2Dt96DBLbjBZ
QmRzjt7qTql1bMdoJDwsC6ZnDX1PW1vTiav1xewHYAPJNT
QmaCpDMGvV2BGHeYERUEnRQAwe3N8SzbUtfsmvsqQLuvuJ
QmepsDPxWtLDuKvEoafkpJxGij4kMax11uTH7WnKqD25Dq
QmUy5jHXui2KzZRC3ofzHKYGmJVqAJTCsRRo2EZ6Wzwee7
```

Peers are identified by their default peerID generated by IPFS. Let's examine how we got them in *app.go*. Notice how the method `displayUsers` is called when the user routes to `/discover`. Our first step is to get all the peers from IPFS:

```
//get peers
peers := node.Peerstore.Peers()
data := make([]string, len(peers))
for i := range data {
    // assuming little endian
data[i] = peer.IDB58Encode(peers[i])
}
fmt.Println("the peers are %s", data)
```

We pull all the peers from the peerstore; internally, this is the `IPFS swarm peers` command. Next, we create an array the length of peers and iterate through it. We use the method `IDB58Encode` to encode the peers to a pretty string that we can parse and store each one of them in the data array. Then, we pass the array back to the frontend of the discover.html page. The discover.html page is very similar to the user home page. It's just a dynamically sized HTML table that fills in all the posts for the specified peer. The only difference is that it passes in the peer list array instead of the post's array:

```
var arr = [
{{range .Allpeers}}
{{.}},
{{end}}
    ];
```

Dapp Economics

Now comes the fun part. Let's turn this little dapp into its own micro economy. Recall the discussion of ideal forms of money in Chapter 3. Colored coins is currently the best solution for issuing assets within your dapp. You don't want to have to deal with the pain and annoyance of bootstrapping a blockchain just so you can have your own appcoin. It's not worth it when the Bitcoin blockchain already exists with its 500-plus supercomputer computing power worth of Sybil resistance. Although Counterparty offers a valuable solution, it introduces a new currency to the mold, unnecessarily complicating things, and doesn't offer modularity of features. With colored coins, we can create an asset on the Bitcoin blockchain that is owned by no one and fluctuate in value with the value of the dapp itself.

So, how do we create our own set of colored coins? I've found the website Coinprism (*http://www.coinprism.com*) to be the easiest current solution. Coinprism is an online colored coins wallet. You can create your own account and you'll be taken to the main wallet page. Creating a colored coin requires a fee of 0.0001 BTC. This is currently a necessary evil, until some service comes along and takes on the fee, kind of like Onename did for Namecoin identities. I went ahead and transferred 0.0005 BTC from coinbase to my colored coin wallet.

Then, you go to Addresses and Transactions → Create a New Color Address. The website will prompt you to create an address, as shown in Figure 3-2.

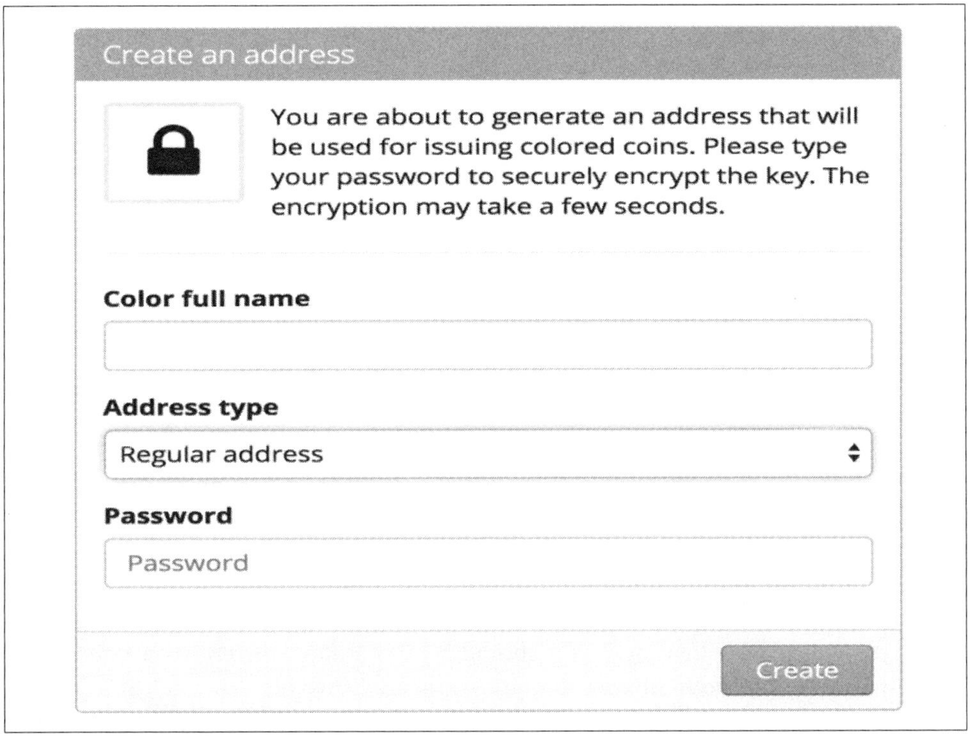

Create an address

🔒 You are about to generate an address that will be used for issuing colored coins. Please type your password to securely encrypt the key. The encryption may take a few seconds.

Color full name

[   ]

Address type

[Regular address   ⬍]

Password

[Password   ]

[Create]

Figure 3-2. Create an address

Name your coin; most usually end with the word "coin," but it's not mandatory. Your coin could even double as the name of your app. like the WhatsApp competitor Gems. I chose a regular address because I don't want to deal with offline storage.

Next, transfer coins from your main address to the new address. Now with this new address, you can issue colored coins to yourself. Your main address will store both Bitcoins and colored coins. The fee is 0.001 BTC, and you can choose an arbitrary number of shares to be associated with the colored coins. I chose 100,000 (as shown in Figure 3-3), but you can choose a million if you'd like. It's better to err on the bigger side of numbers so that you'll have enough coins to go around if your dapp gets really big.

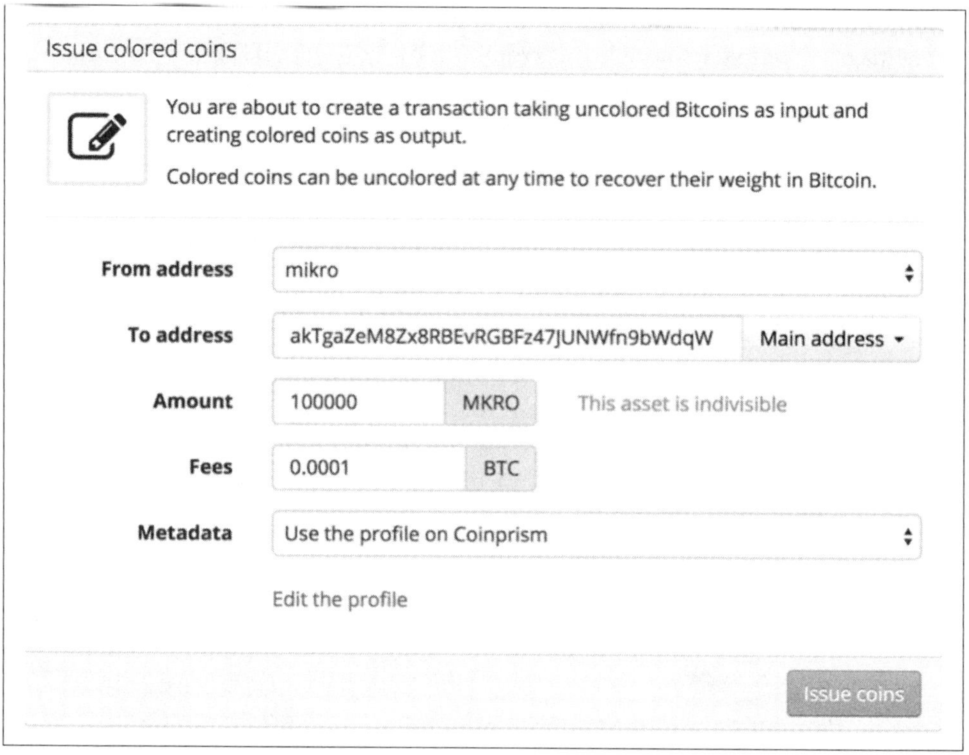

Figure 3-3. Issue colored coins

When the transaction has been completed, the new address will have all X shares of dapp coins you've just created, as demonstrated in Figure 3-4.

After you've finished that step, you should see your new currency on your wallet home page, next to your Bitcoin amount. Congrats! You now own all of the assets you've just created. Think of them as shares in your dapp startup. You can give them away to whomever you want, and as the valuation of your startup increases, so will the valuation of your shares. No more waiting for IPOs to become a public company.

These assets remove the barriers to entry for users to benefit and profit from using your dapp. It will incentivize users to grow the network as necessary to continue to gain assets to access scarce resources in the network; in this case, those scarce resources would be posts.

Figure 3-4. Your wallet

So how do we structure our Mikro economy? Do we charge users to make a post? We could, but to whom would the money go? Most likely, it would go to whatever nodes offer a third-party storage solution for our (encrypted) data. But for now, because we don't have a system like that yet in IPFS, we will make it free to post, pay to view. That means a user can make as many posts as he likes for free, but to view other users' posts, he'll need to pay the author of the post a small, preset amount of coins. That way, users will be paid for outputting data to the network, and they can use the money they earn to either view other tweets, or spend it on outside expenses.

Kerala isn't just a wrapper for IPFS, it also makes sending transactions easy with just a single function call. Recall that in the `TextInput` method called on all profile pages, that if a profile page is loaded that has posts and belongs to another user, this function is called:

```
hash := kerala.Pay("1000","1HihKUXo6UEjJzm4DZ9oQFPu2uVc9YK9Wh",
"akSjSW57xhGp86K6JFXXroACfRCw7SPv637", "10",
"AHthB6AQHaSS9VffkfMqTKTxVV43Dgst36",
"L1jftH241t2rhQSTrru9Vd2QumX4VuGsPhVfSPvibc4TYU4aGdaa" )
```

This function pays the user profile page that you are viewing a set amount to view all of the user's posts and returns the transaction hash for your records.

The parameters of the pay method are as follows:

```
Pay(fee string, from_address string, to_address string, amount string, asset_id
    string, private_key string) (string)
```

`fee string`
> This is the required fee to send a transaction.

`from_address`
> This is your asset address.

`to_address`
> This is asset address of the user whose post you want to read.

`amount string`
> This is how much you want user A to pay user B to access user B's posts.

`asset_id string`
> This the ID of the asset that the dapp owner has created.

Right now, all cryptocurrency-related data is dealing with the test version of the Coinprism API. When you are ready for production, you can change this to the production version of the API, and the docs on Coinprism (*http://bit.ly/coinprism-docs*) make it simple. (You just switch out the test URL to the production URL in Kerala.)

The pay method creates a transaction, takes the unsigned response, and calculates its hex value. Then, it signs the hex value and pushes it to the network. The returned value is the hash of the transaction that you can verify on the Bitcoin blockchain. Sending cryptocurrency transactions is more painful than it should be to do from scratch, so I thought abstracting it all to one method would be useful.

There is one more method called `GenerateAddress`. For your dapp, you can set it so `GenerateAddress` is called when a user first runs the app so that he has his own asset address from which to send and receive funds.

Remaining Problems

There are still some issues not implemented in this demo, but all of them are possible and the dapp will likely be updated over time. I welcome any contributions.

Private Networks

You'll notice that in this demo dapp, there are no friends. You have a profile, can discover other users, and see their posts after paying them, but you can't "friend" them in the traditional sense of a social network. Friending someone requires data encryption. The idea is that your DAG is encrypted with a public-private keypair, and only those nodes that you trust on the network can gain access to your private keypair to unlock and view your data. If you unfriend someone, the app can generate a new public-private keypair and rebroadcast the private key to all of your remaining friends. This way, the old friend won't still have access to your data. So where is this functionality? It's called IPFS Keystore, and it's still under development. By the time you get this book, it will most likely be done, and will be a simple matter of implementing a few extra lines of code. You can find the specification at *https://github.com/ipfs/specs/tree/master/keystore*.

Human-Readable Names

The peerIDs on the discover page are not very pretty. They're unique, but they're not human readable. Recall earlier in the book that we mentioned Namecoin as the technology completing Zooko's Triangle and letting you create decentralized, human-readable, and secure names. Because peerIDs are already unique, you can prompt users to register a human-readable name on the Namecoin blockchain and then associate their peerID with their Namecoin name. Whenever you view data authored by a user, the app can verify that user's identity by verifying on the Namecoin blockchain whether the user's peerID sent the registration transaction for their Namecoin identity. An alternative is to create a web-of-trust within the app like a reputation system. Of course, the easiest alternative is to use a name shortening service (a centralized namespace), but it would introduce a central point of failure. My preferred method is Namecoin.

Showing Only Peers on Mikro, Not IPFS in General

The discover page shows all peers on the IPFS network instead of just peers who are using Mikro. As IPNS matures, this will become easier to accomplish, but we can set a file like *app.config* in our IPNS namespace and users looking for others can just iterate through the network and check whether each node has a Mikro-specific signature in our file. If they do, the node will be listed on the discovery page.

Tamper-Free Payments

In our code, we made a payment to a user via the `Pay()` method in Kerala before pulling the user's data from IPFS. What if a bad user just removed that little `Pay()` snippet from the source code before accessing the node's data? It's entirely possible to do. Each user can have a listener running that waits for a payment to occur to their asset address. If a payment occurs, then and only then does the client send the payment sender a copy of the user's private key to access her data. To get the asset address of another user, your dapp could store it as the first entry in its own publicly accessible DAG.

Where do smart contracts play into all this? Namecoin has its own smart contracts for name registration built in. Since Ethereum's inception, Bitcoin's core developers have learned a lot of lessons and made the scripting language more complete to allow for a wide range of applications, and this is one of them. Ethereum made some great research contributions to blockchain technology, but the unfortunate truth for them is that when it comes to decentralized apps, most often global consensus just isn't necessary and proves to be too expensive.

Blockchains are really good at dealing with financial assets, but computation and storage are out of the question. An example of when you would use a smart contract is as a third-party escrow service. Funds would live on the blockchain until the deal was complete and would receive notice to be released to the specified address. This dapp didn't require use of one, but we'll see use cases later on.

And that's it! You have just built and run your first dapp from source. Feel free to use it as a starting point to build your own profitable, open source startup.

## CHAPTER 4

OpenBazaar

This chapter will take a deep dive into the decentralized market, OpenBazaar (*https:// openbazaar.org*). We'll discuss the rationale and overall structure of the transactions it supports and then talk through implementing an OpenBazaar instance as well as its potential next steps and flaws.

Why Make OpenBazaar?

Bitcoin really got people excited about developing next-generation ecommerce with speedy micropayments and better security. The first institutions to utilize Bitcoin at a large scale were centralized providers like Overstock and Dish Network. Bitcoin provided these mainstream companies with an opportunity to showcase their tech savvy, but its pseudonymity and immediate value transfer were much more suited to a marketplace for illegal goods: Silk Road.

Silk Road was like the underground version of eBay. It was a centralized website, but to gain access to it you had to use *onion routing* via Tor. The creator made it very difficult for casual users to access it, and it was considered the pinnacle of the "dark web." People primarily bought and sold illegal drugs on Silk Road, particularly in jurisdictions with strict antidrug laws. Although part of Silk Road's business might have been universally repugnant, other sales involved cross-jurisdictional sales of "light" drugs like marijuana (and even tobacco) or nondrug items like erotic art and books, jewelry, and the like.

It all worked out for quite a while, but eventually the United States government caught up with Silk Road because it had a central point of failure: all of its data was stored on a single server. So, when the government seized the server, Silk Road was taken down and all of the users lost their data associated with the website. Another user tried restarting the site as Silk Road 2.0; eventually the feds caught up with him as well, and the site was shut down for a second time.

Pirate Bay is in a similar position; however, given the relatively less serious level of illegality it enables, the government response has been commensurately less permanent. The site has been taken down multiple times by multiple government organizations, and yet it just keeps popping up. The site owners simply plan on the fly where they next want their server to be after it's been taken down. Clearly this isn't a long-term solution, but there is a very high-value need for people to get things that are otherwise impossible for them because of the law.

Aside from the technical vulnerability, the other point of failure for marketplace apps has been the leader in charge with access to all the data. The arrest of Ross Ulbricht, aka the Dread Pirate Roberts, the founder of Silk Road, made headlines around the world. He is now serving life in prison for narcotics trafficking and computer crimes. The need for a decentralized marketplace became more and more apparent after the government's dealings with Silk Road—a marketplace where no single person had administrative access control over the data and that could run locally on anyone's computer. It was out of this need that OpenBazaar was born.

What Is OpenBazaar?

With OpenBazaar, there is no central server involved at all. It's a peer-to-peer client to which no government entity can restrict access. OpenBazaar doesn't operate under the approval of any law; it's the evolution of unrestricted global marketplace. As its creators put it, "It's like eBay and BitTorrent had a baby."

OpenBazaar is a platform that lets buyers and sellers connect directly to sell their goods without involving a third party to host the data and charge a transaction fee. The creators wanted to build on the idea of creating a truly free trade platform for people to send and receive goods without having to go through a central authority. The Internet has never really hosted anything like the bazaars of the past: peer-to-peer marketplaces where buyers and sellers could interact directly with one another without anyone between observing the transaction. OpenBazaar hopes to bring that concept to the Internet.

The developers won a hackathon in Toronto for their project called DarkMarket. It has since been renamed OpenBazaar and they have many developers on the team now. They mostly receive funds in the form of donations from people. They don't really profit from this, and that's one major flaw in this dapp: without incentivizing network members, this business plan doesn't scale. The flaw could be mitigated by introducing a metacoin that would increase in value instead of using Bitcoin directly.

How Does OpenBazaar Work?

Everyone in the OpenBazaar network is a node in the P2P network. Everyone is assigned three roles that they can build on: merchant, buyer, and/or arbiter. You can choose what role you mainly want to build your reputation for, and you are not limited to one role. The currency presently in use is Bitcoin, removing the barrier to entry of having to deal with a novel currency—but this also doesn't let the developers automatically be paid for their work. Let's talk about what the process looks like for each of these three types of actors in the network.

Merchant

OpenBazaar's interface is still under development, but all of the basic elements necessary for the site to function in alpha are in place. Merchants only need to go to the setting tab and type a nickname for their store. They also input their profile image, Bitcoin address, and Namecoin ID (optional). After they've filled out their credentials (see Figure 4-1), they can save it, with the data being saved locally to their computers.

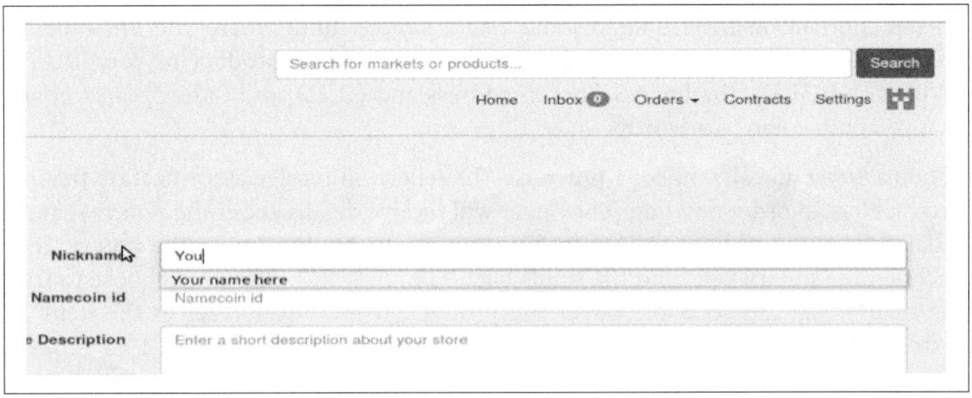

Figure 4-1. OpenBazaar credentials interface example

Merchants also have the ability to communicate with their buyers, either directly on OpenBazaar using a messaging protocol built on ZeroMQ or by using a third-party communication protocol like email, bitmessage, or their own website. Because OpenBazaar is currently in alpha phase, updates to the protocol can delete a merchant's store data. As a result, the developers created a backup option that lets merchants create a backup of their store data that they can easily reintegrate in case of data loss.

The interesting part comes when merchants list their goods on OpenBazaar. It uses the concept of Ricardian contracts (*http://bit.ly/ricardian*) to facilitate trade on the network. This is different from smart contracts because they don't live on a blockchain; instead, they live on the merchant's computer. A Ricardian contract is basically a way to track the liability of Party A when selling goods to Party B. It represents a single unit of a good. These contracts are used in the dapp to track legitimately signed agreements between both parties, and these agreements can't be forged after the contract has been signed (Figure 4-2).

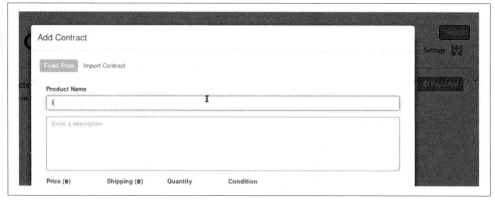

Figure 4-2. Adding a contract to OpenBazaar via the user interface

So the contract on the frontend looks like a simple input where you enter details about your product and price. Additionally, it links your product to your Bitcoin address and GUID, the buyer's Bitcoin address and GUID, and a third-party notary that you both deem trustworthy.

When a buyer actually makes a purchase, the seller will receive a notification that her product has an order pending. The buyer will receive details about the notary that the seller has trusted to hold the funds. The buyer can choose to trust the notary. If he declines, the notary will send the funds back to him. If the seller does choose to trust the notary, she can send the buyer the product. If the buyer receives the item, he instructs the notary to send the funds to the seller. If the buyer doesn't do this, the notary will act as a dispute resolution party, and after compiling information from both sides, will decide as to which party is most likely telling the truth.

Buyer

Buyers type in their credentials in the same fashion as the merchant, but they have the duty of selecting a notary. Buyers select the notary, but it's the sellers who can accept or decline the validity and reputation of said notary. As of this writing, this dapp is in its early days, and building trust and reputation requires time, so it's best for people to only make small transactions in case notaries are bad actors. Eventually quality notaries will rise to the top—perhaps people will create notary services as businesses and they will become the most-trusted and dominant players.

Notary

Anyone can be a notary by simply turning on a checkbox in their profile. Whenever a buyer adds a party as a notary for their purchase contract, the notary can receive funds, mitigate disputes, and send funds to the rightful party. Notaries can charge a percentage fee for providing dispute resolution. If both selling and buying parties complete their transaction without needing the assistance of the notary, there is no payment necessary. If the notary is needed to refund the buyer or engage in dispute resolution, the notary will receive a percentage from the multisig. Notaries publicly display their fee under the services tab in their "storefront."

Currently, notaries automatically accept all transactions that assign them as a notary, but eventually they'll be able to screen transactions and have the ability to accept or decline them. We can see in Figure 4-3 that the basic functionality is there. Figure 4-4 shows a completed order.

Figure 4-3. The notary interface for OpenBazaar

Figure 4-4. Order example of a handmade pipe

How to Install OpenBazaar

Now that I've talked about what OpenBazaar is and how it works, let's download it and give it a whirl ourselves. We'll talk about it from a technical standpoint, look at the pros and cons of the technologies the developers decided to use in the stack, and discuss the way they've decided to design this dapp.

As of this writing, there is no binary here, so you need to build from source.

First you're going to need to install Python. If you're running the latest version of OS X, it comes with Python 2.7 installed out of the box. Otherwise, you'll need to install it manually via Homebrew. Homebrew is like the missing "apt-get" feature from Linux for OS X. I've found it supremely useful when compiling dapps from source, because there is almost always at least one missing-dependency error.

To install Homebrew, in the Terminal, type the following:

```
ruby -e "$(curl -fsSL
https://raw.githubusercontent.com/Homebrew/install/master/install
Homebrew/install/master/in
```

From then on, you can easily install thousands of packages by using this format:

```
brew install _____
```

OpenBazaar was built using Python. It's a solid object-oriented language that has amassed a huge number of useful libraries over the years, with many distributed projects like RPyc being built with it, so using it is not a bad choice at all.

You're also going to need to install Pip, Python's module installer:

```
Brew install pip
```

Now, you can build OpenBazaar from source:

```
git clone https://github.com/OpenBazaar/OpenBazaar.git

cd OpenBazaar

./configure.sh

./OpenBazaar start
```

Possible Errors

The following is a collection of errors you might encounter as you build this code locally on your own machine. Keep in mind that this is still actively in development, so things might break.

Dependencies

You might get some dependency errors, given that this project is under development. Don't be surprised to receive messages similar to "X wasn't found." You can just systematically install each dependency manually using Homebrew as they come up. So if you get an error, locate the dependency, Brew-install it, and then retry `./OpenBazaar start`. A new dependency error might come up. Just keep repeating until all the necessary dependencies are installed and then it will run.

Ports

You might see the following error:

```
1. If you are using VPN, configure port forwarding or
disable your VPN temporarily
2. Configure your router to forward traffic from port 62112 for both TCP and UDP
to your local port 62112
```

This means that one of the ports that OpenBazaar is trying to use is blocked by either a firewall or your router. Ensure that those ports can be accessed in your system and router settings.

Data Storage and Retrieval

Data isn't stored on a DHT in OpenBazaar; it's stored locally in a SQLite datastore at each node. In *datastore.py*, we can see the `set_item` method that takes a key-value pair as input with some timestamps and credentials. It inserts the pair into the database as its own entry locally on the user's computer. Here's the code in OpenBazaar that does that:

```python
def set_item(self, key, value, last_published, originally_published,
             original_publisher_id, market_id=1):

    rows = self.db_connection.select_entries(
        "datastore",
        {"key": key,
         "market_id": market_id}
    )
    if len(rows) == 0:
        self.db_connection.insert_entry(
            "datastore",
            {
                'key': key,
                'value': value,
                'lastPublished': last_published,
                'originallyPublished': originally_published,
                'originalPublisherID': original_publisher_id,
                'market_id': market_id
            }
        )
```

```
        else:
            self.db_connection.update_entries(
                "datastore",
                {
                    'key': key,
                    'value': value,
                    'lastPublished': last_published,
                    'originallyPublished': originally_published,
                    'originalPublisherID': original_publisher_id,
                    'market_id': market_id
                },
                {
                    'key': key,
                    'market_id': market_id
                }
            )
```

You can then query these values by using the db_query method:

```
def _db_query(self, key, column_name):

    row = self.db_connection.select_entries("datastore", {"key": key})

    if len(row) != 0:
        value = row[0][column_name]
        try:
            value = ast.literal_eval(value)
        except Exception:
            pass
        return value
```

This only needs a key to retrieve the necessary value as well as the column name—which doubles as the publisher_id.

OpenBazaar does use a DHT, but not for data storage. The DHT in OpenBazaar was inspired by Kademlia (like BitTorrent and IPFS) and is used as a sort of "yellow pages" for peers. It's a decentralized index of peers that instructs every node how to contact every other node for the sake of selling and sharing Ricardian contracts. When two nodes connect via the DHT each node can pull data from the other directly:

```
def __init__(self, market_id, key, call="findNode", callback=None):
    self.key = key
    # Key to search for
    self.call = call
    # Either findNode or findValue depending on search
    self.callback = callback
    # Callback for when search finishes
    self.shortlist = []
    # List of nodes that are being searched against
    self.active_probes = []
    #
```

```
self.already_contacted = []
# Nodes are added to this list when they've been sent a findXXX action
self.previous_closest_node = None
# This is updated to be the closest node found during search
self.find_value_result = {}
# If a find_value search is found this is the value
self.slow_node_count = [0]
#
self.contacted_now = 0
# Counter for how many nodes have been contacted
self.prev_shortlist_length = 0

self.log = logging.getLogger(
    '[%s] %s' % (market_id, self.__class__.__name__)
)

# Create a unique ID (SHA1) for this iterative_find request to support
parallel searches
self.find_id = hashlib.sha1(os.urandom(128)).hexdigest()
```

In the file *node/DHT.py*, under the class `DHTSearch`, the init method helps search through the DHT for other nodes about which you want to get more data. It assumes that you know the key of the node so that lookup time is faster, but in OpenBazaar's DHT, it acts like a broadcasts for every node so brute-force discovery is also possible.

OpenBazaar's designers have structured all relevant user data to be sent as a JSON object called `data` in `proto_page` under *protocol.py*:

```
def proto_page(uri, pubkey, guid, text, signature, nickname, PGPPubKey, email,
               bitmessage, arbiter, notary, notary_description, notary_fee,
               arbiter_description, sin, homepage, avatar_url):
    data = {
        'type': 'page',
        'uri': uri,
        'pubkey': pubkey,
        'senderGUID': guid,
        'text': text,
        'nickname': nickname,
        'PGPPubKey': PGPPubKey,
        'email': email,
        'bitmessage': bitmessage,
        'arbiter': arbiter,
        'notary': notary,
        'notary_description': notary_description,
        'notary_fee': notary_fee,
        'arbiter_description': arbiter_description,
        'sin': sin,
        'homepage': homepage,
        'avatar_url': avatar_url,
        'v': constants.VERSION
    }
    return data
```

This data is sent and retrieved between users identifying one another after they have been found in the DHT.

Another great thing about the DHT is that we can also search by keyword. Because keywords are user-defined in their storefronts, they can be product related or category related, making search easier and more user-friendly:

```
def find_listings_by_keyword(self, keyword, listing_filter=None, callback=None):

        hashvalue = hashlib.new('ripemd160')
        keyword_key = 'keyword-%s' % keyword
        hashvalue.update(keyword_key.encode('utf-8'))
        listing_index_key = hashvalue.hexdigest()

        self.log.info('Finding contracts for keyword: %s', keyword)

        self.iterative_find_value(listing_index_key, callback)
```

Like IPFS, OpenBazaar uses a DHT. Unlike IPFS, OpenBazaar doesn't accommodate data replication via content-addressed data; no matter how many people want it, the data will only live locally on the originating computer. As is logical for a system that doesn't rely on distributing copies of the data, there also is no versioning of the data built in.

Identity

Nodes in OpenBazaar have their own unique GUID. This is similar to IPFS nodes with their peerIDs:

```
Under node/transport.py

 def _generate_new_keypair(self):

        seed = str(random.randrange(2 ** 256))

        # Move to BIP32 keys m/0/0/0
        wallet = bitcoin.bip32_ckd(bitcoin.bip32_master_key(seed), 0)
        wallet_chain = bitcoin.bip32_ckd(wallet, 0)
        bip32_identity_priv = bitcoin.bip32_ckd(wallet_chain, 0)
        identity_priv = bitcoin.bip32_extract_key(bip32_identity_priv)
        bip32_identity_pub = bitcoin.bip32_privtopub(bip32_identity_priv)
        identity_pub =
bitcoin.encode_pubkey(bitcoin.bip32_extract_key(bip32_identity_pub), 'hex')

        self.pubkey = identity_pub
        self.secret = identity_priv

        # Generate SIN
        sha_hash = hashlib.sha256()
        sha_hash.update(self.pubkey)
        ripe_hash = hashlib.new('ripemd160')
```

```
        ripe_hash.update(sha_hash.digest())

        self.guid = ripe_hash.hexdigest()
```

These identities are generated via Bitcoin's BIP32 (hierarchical deterministic wallets) protocol by generating a new SIN using SHA-256 to create your GUID. The GUID is as unique as each Bitcoin address is unique so we don't have to worry about duplicates.

So, we're able to give unique identities to people, just like in IPFS, by using the elliptic-curve technology behind Bitcoin, but how do we make them human-readable? OpenBazaar also has an input credential for your Namecoin ID as an additional identity field besides your self-assigned nickname. Thus, people basically can have duplicate nicknames and the GUID can be used to validate which one is which. This is suboptimal: perhaps you can memorize the last five digits of someone's GUID as well as their username. But Namecoin makes up for this flaw by making it possible for users to also have a Namecoin ID:

```
def is_valid_Namecoin(Namecoin, guid):
    if not Namecoin or not guid:
        return False

    server = DNSChainServer.Server(constants.DNSCHAIN_SERVER_IP, "")
    _log.info("Looking up Namecoin id: %s", Namecoin)
    try:
        data = server.lookup("id/" + Namecoin)
    except (DNSChainServer.DataNotFound, DNSChainServer.MalformedJSON):
        _log.info('Claimed remote Namecoin id not found: %s', Namecoin)
        return False

    return data.get('OpenBazaar') == guid
```

The code checks against DNSChain to see if the Namecoin ID is valid every time by checking whether that GUID is stored in the Namecoin address of the person claiming the identity. DNSChain is a hybrid DNS server for easy access to Namecoin data via an API.

So OpenBazaar's identity problem is solved through a combination of uniquely generated GUID's and Namecoin, similar to IPFS.

Reputation

But what about reputation? Reputation is a big part of any marketplace environment; buyers want to be able to trust sellers, and vice versa. In a centralized model, server-owners can hand out reputation to individuals and, with appropriate security, they don't need to deal with individuals tampering with their own reputation to defraud the system. In a decentralized system, reputation is much more difficult to verify.

Trust is dealt with in OpenBazaar through two different types of synergistic systems: *global trust* and *projected trust*. When all members of the network trust a particular user of the network in the same way, this is called global trust. This trust is established through *proof-of-burn* and *proof-of-timelock*. Projected trust is trust directed toward a certain node, which might be different for each user of the network. So the trust is projected from each user to the node. This trust is established through a pseudonymous partial knowledge web of trust.

Let's look at each of these methods in more detail.

Method 1: proof-of-burn

When a seller creates a store, he must spend Bitcoin that is lost and never returns. This makes it expensive for a user to create multiple identities and is the fundamental Sybil-attack prevention mechanism in OpenBazaar. Though not perfect, it is a deterrent. The larger the proof-of-burn, the more expensive it is to make an account, but the higher the barrier to entry for potential players is to use the service. Publicly and verifiably burning some coins in a set-limit currency is *remurrage* on the remainder. Remurrage is the opposite of demurrage (the cost of holding currency over a given period). Suppose that you are sitting at home on your laptop and create a currency with 10 million coins that people begin trading instantly. When you go out for a walk and come back, there are now only 5 million issued coins that aren't burned. If you're holding any of that currency, it's the equivalent of receiving a dividend on top of the general economy-tracking price that we've grown to expect from a set-quantity currency like Bitcoin.

The dapp first generates a burn address directly from a node's GUID:

```
def burnaddr_from_guid(guid_hex):
    _log.debug("burnaddr_from_guid: %s", guid_hex)

    prefix = '6f' if TESTNET else '00'
    guid_full_hex = prefix + guid_hex
    _log.debug("GUID address on bitcoin net: %s", guid_full_hex)

    # Perturbate GUID to ensure unspendability through
    # near-collision resistance of SHA256 by flipping
    # the last non-checksum bit of the address.
    guid_full = guid_full_hex.decode('hex')
    guid_prt = guid_full[:-1] + chr(ord(guid_full[-1]) ^ 1)
    addr_prt = obelisk.bitcoin.EncodeBase58Check(guid_prt)
    _log.debug("Perturbated bitcoin proof-of-burn address: %s", addr_prt)

    return addr_prt
```

From there it's just a simple transaction on the GUID. All nodes can verify that a certain GUID has burned coins (proof-of-burn) by performing the same `burnadd_from_guid` function on the guid hex and verifying its burn amount on the blockchain.

Method 2: proof-of-timelock

Proof-of-burn lets the network create identities such that it is costly to recreate. Proof-of-timelock, by rendering a particular amount of coin unspendable for a time (and tying a user identity to that unspent coin as a "deposit"), ensures that it's impossible that a huge number of real-world identities associated with one real-world entity can simultaneously exist at any specific moment in time. Proof-of-timelock is not as strong an insurance as proof-of-burn: proof-of-burn is, effectively, permanent proof-of-timelock.

In proof-of-timelock, the node that wants to establish trust toward a pseudonymous identity must provably lock a specified amount of currency inside a transaction that gives the currency back to them eventually. The transaction has the feature that it isn't executed for a specified amount of time. The network knows that the transaction will take place eventually, the amount of it, and the amount of time it will remain locked. All of these things are publicly verifiable.

One of the main appeals of proof-of-timelock is psychological: it just feels less guilty than proof-of-burn. There is a certain psychological burden associated with money destruction and it might not be an easy one to overcome. People will most likely use it more often than proof-of-burn.

The Bitcoin blockchain currently doesn't allow for a proof-of-timelock mechanism directly. Although the Bitcoin protocol supports the `nLockTime` value, the mechanism is not currently honored by running nodes. This means that the transaction won't be broadcast in a publicly verifiable way.

This would be a perfect use case for the Ethereum blockchain because it allows for Turing-complete smart contracts. OpenBazaar decided to avoid using it though because it hasn't proven feasible in practice and has a lot of problems in terms of scalability and performance. This was a smart decision and the sidechain proposal will mitigate some of this risk eventually.

Method 3: trust-as-risk (most viable)

The developers are still working out the details of the web-of-trust model and how to actually implement it programmatically, but it seems like they are heading in the direction of using trust-as-risk. They've been toying with the idea of letting people extend others a line of credit if the creditor trusts the party to whom it is extending it. So the idea would be that if you really trust someone, you can give them 0.1 Bitcoin in a line of credit via a multisignature transaction; if you stop trusting them, you can withdraw your line of credit.

The indicators for trust need to be hosted persistently in a decentralized way. Because the OpenBazaar developers don't want to add to blockchain bloat on Bitcoin (always a good train of thought), they are leaning toward using Namecoin as a good alternative. I find this to be a really reasonable approach.

They could end up not even implementing a web-of-trust because it might not even matter that much. In real life, when someone tries to scam us and we lose money, we can just call our banks to cancel a trade and recover the funds. In the OpenBazaar network, a notary is the key intermediary in transactions and has the potential to prevent a scam from occurring the first place. Nodes could just place all of their trust with them rather than other peers. It will be interesting to see how trust plays out in the network, but a web-of-trust to me seems like a necessary addition to secure the network.

What Could OpenBazaar Have Done Better?

To begin with, the most important flaw here is the lack of an internal currency. Bitcoin provides immediate liquidity, and that is good for sellers, but having an internal currency is a win-win situation for early adopters and the developers themselves. First of all, using OpenBazaar is a risk for early adopters anyway, given that their Bitcoin can be stolen because of the lack of reputable notaries and reputation takes time to build. It would be better if OpenBazaar issued its own currency that would be used to make purchases inside the dapp. OpenBazaar would have a crowd sale and set an initial price of the currency and set a limited number of tokens.

These coins would be colored coins, so they could set up a Bitcoin contract address (aka send-coins-here) which would calculate how many OBcoins you get in return to send to the OpenBazaar address you specify. As OpenBazaar grows in valuation, the values of the coins would rise. OpenBazaaar early adopters would be rewarded for their efforts in bootstrapping the network despite the risk, liquidity would increase for buyers and sellers, and, most important, the developers of the open source software would be paid for their work. Funding is one of the major competitive advantages of centralized closed-source software over open source. The former simply is able to pay top developers to maintain and upgrade the app, but with an internal currency, we can bring that model to open source software.

One other questionable choice is OpenBazaar's data storage model: just storing it in a local SQLite datastore with no redundancy or replication. If they used IPFS for data storage, it would be more resilient. The more people that visited a store, the more copies of that store's data there would be. Store owners could get a notice of how many other people were replicating their encrypted store data for peace of mind.

The knowledge of how OpenBazaar was built (and the constraints it was built under) with its flaws and successes can play into the design of many types of apps. We'll see some of the same themes pop up in our next case study: Lighthouse.

## CHAPTER 5

Lighthouse

Mike Hearn was a Bitcoin core developer for over five years and has gained a lot of respect in the community for the work he's done with BitcoinJ (a Java-based Bitcoin SDK) and his Bitcoin talks worldwide. His latest project is called Lighthouse (*https:// www.vinumeris.com/lighthouse*); it aims to decentralize crowdfunding. Hearn felt that crowdfunding sites like Kickstarter and Indiegogo take too large a cut of project funding for their work in server maintenance, advertising, hosting, and moderation of crowdfunding projects submitted to them. Add on additional payment processing fees like Stripe or Amazon Payments, and up to 10 percent of whatever money you've raised is gone. Lighthouse is an attempt to cut out the middleman so that fundraisers can get all of the money their supporters intend to give them.

Furthermore, there are geographic limitations on Kickstarter. On that site, project creation is currently only available to people in North America, New Zealand, and Europe. This means project creation on Kickstarter is impossible for the vast majority of the planet. As a practical matter, jurisdictions that don't allow crowdfunding can ban sites like Kickstarter because they are IP addressed.

On top of that, there are certain projects that are impossible to create on Kickstarter because of the rules that the site imposes as a central authority in the name of community standards. This is not limited to centralized funding sites: though controversial, decentralized moderation is possible by embedding blacklists into the blockchain via majority or delegated votes by nodes that all nodes must accept.

Allowing for crowdfunding without taking deposits was another motivation because deposits taken in a decentralized app are a very risky proposition. A lot of security issues can arise but theoretically the Bitcoin protocol allows for a middle ground of revocability, and Lighthouse was perhaps the first app to implement a little-known feature in the protocol that allowed for just that.

thouse is a good case study in smart contracts, as well. It probably isn't consid-
...u a killer app, but it is approaching that vicinity of actual utility because you get
more money in your pocket as a fundraiser. It also features speedier payments
because of how lightweight Bitcoin is compared to other payment processors. The
barrier to entry for any fundraiser goes to zero and payments move at the speed of the
protocol without requiring the approval of banks in the middle.

Functionality

The easiest way to test out Lighthouse is to just go to the website (*https://www.vinume
ris.com/lighthouse*), and download the binary correlating with your specific operating
system. Next, double-click the lighthouse icon to open the introduction page, as
shown in Figure 5-1.

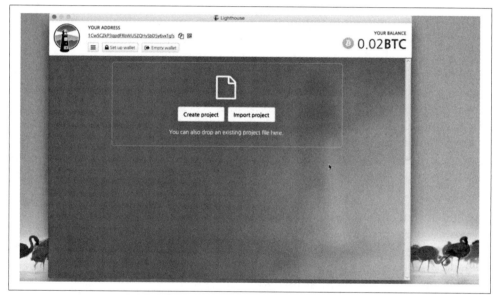

Figure 5-1. Lighthouse main page

On the the introduction page, you can choose between creating a project or import-
ing one. There is no app discovery page (we'll explain why later). You can drag an
existing project onto the page and it will show up in its full layout format so that you
can add funds to it (Figure 5-2).

Or, you can go ahead and pledge your own amount of money to the project, as depic-
ted in Figure 5-3.

You can add your Bitcoin balance to Lighthouse and fund projects with it. You can
get your deposit refunded at any time without risk of losing your money if the project
hasn't reached its goals and the creator hasn't collected the funds. You can also start

your own project and advertise it yourself on social media. Other people will download your project file and fund it themselves.

Figure 5-2. An example of a lighthouse crowdsource fund

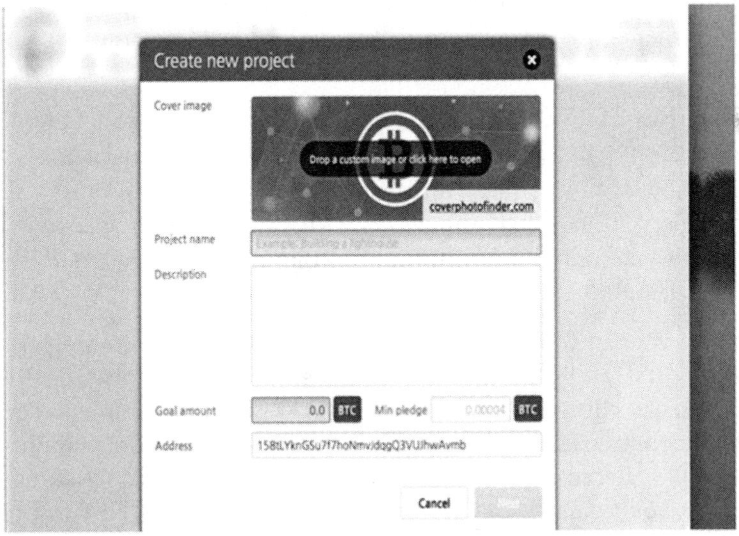

Figure 5-3. Create new project

The first thought you might have is how inefficient it is to be forced to import and export project files instead of having a discovery page in the app, kind of like the

Mikro app from Chapter 3. Lighthouse's creator decided to avoid it, simply because it's too difficult to do. It adds complexity and bugs and he didn't have enough money or time to do that. Decentralized system development is difficult, and bugs arise that would never come up in centralized systems. Bugs related to UI synchronization and state management are very difficult to debug; for example, "I clicked a button and now I see all pledges twice, and then I restarted the app and now it's fixed." UI synchronization bugs happen in Lighthouse despite not even sharing data in a P2P network.

IPFS would've been great here, had Hearn known about it. It could've been used as a module to share files between nodes. It isn't as expensive as Bitcoin and it has the speed of BitTorrent, the versioning of Git, and the reliability that comes with having a content-addressed system where data is replicated by everyone who requests it. Even if IPFS wasn't used, any Kademlia-based DHT would've been great, but again we come up against the problem that has historically plagued decentralized software development: lack of funds. An internal currency would help solve this problem, but we can talk about that at the end of the chapter.

Instead, users have the option to utilize a server to transfer files. They can host files on a network of federated servers that run Lighthouse nodes and can store the files. They can use their own personal storage solution like Dropbox or Google Drive and give people links to those files over social media. Most recently, a service called Light-list has popped up; it acts as a server to host all Lighthouse projects. There will likely be a lot of competition in the space, and this is good because there won't be one server to rule them all; rather, there will be several options, and that means more decentralization.

An interesting part of Lighthouse is that it uses a Bitcoin feature that has been available since Bitcoin 0.1 but seems to have been entirely overlooked: SIGHASH_ANYONE CANPAY. Lighthouse was perhaps the first project to ever implement this feature, which allows users to tag their signatures with an annotation that says it's OK for other people to take part in this payment. SIGHASH_ANYONECANPAY lets you merge transactions together into one big transaction.

When you sign your Bitcoin transaction with your private key, nothing can be edited. And that's why it's safe to broadcast that transaction to everyone on the network, because no one can edit your transaction in any way. A Lighthouse pledge is thus an incomplete Bitcoin transaction that takes money from your wallet and puts it into the fundraiser's wallet. Because a transaction that creates money out of thin air breaks the rules of Bitcoin (only miners can create money out of thin air), it won't be complete until everyone pays. With SIGHASH_ANYONECANPAY, if you get enough of these pledges, it will merge them all together and you'll end up with a valid payment that will be merged into the blockchain.

Let's take a look at how Lighthouse is doing this programmatically. We're going to use the Lighthouse repo on GitHub (*https://github.com/vinumeris/lighthouse*) as a programmatic guide; we don't need to clone it and build it from source. We know what it does, so we should dive into how it does it.

Let's first look under the file *PledgingWallet.java*:

```
public PendingPledge createPledge(Project project, Coin value, @Nullable
KeyParameter aesKey,                                        LHProtos.PledgeDetails
details) throws InsufficientMoneyException {
```

This is the function for making a pledge: it encompasses using the SIGHASH_ANYONE CANPAY OP code as well as the first smart contract that we are going to deal with:

```
TransactionOutput stub = findAvailableStub(value);
```

The method takes as a parameter the project in question, its credentials, and the amount that you want to pledge to the project. The code attempts to find a single output that can satisfy the pledge given as a parameter.

Submitting multiple inputs is unfriendly because it increases the fees paid by the pledge claimer. The pledged output is called the stub and the tx that spends it using the SIGHASH_ANYONECANPAY is the pledge. The template tx outputs are the contract:

```
Coin totalFees = Coin.ZERO;
Transaction dependency = null;
if (stub == null) {
final Address stubAddr = currentReceiveKey().toAddress(getParams());
SendRequest req;
if (value.equals(getBalance(BalanceType.AVAILABLE_SPENDABLE)))             req
= SendRequest.emptyWallet(stubAddr);
else
req = SendRequest.to(stubAddr, value);
if (params == UnitTestParams.get())
req.shuffleOutputs = false;
req.aesKey = aesKey;
completeTx(req);
dependency = req.tx;
totalFees = req.fee;
log.info("Created dependency tx {}", dependency.getHash());
 // The change is in a random output position so we have to search for it. It's
possible that there are         // two outputs of the same size, in that case
it doesn't matter which we use.
stub = findOutputOfValue(value, dependency.getOutputs());         if (stub ==
null) {
// We created a dependency tx to make a stub, and now we can't find it. This can
// only happen if we are sending the entire balance and thus had to subtract the
// miner fee from the value.
checkState(req.emptyWallet);
checkState(dependency.getOutputs().size() == 1);
stub = dependency.getOutput(0);
```

```
        }
    }
```

If there is no output like that, then the app tries to create an output of the right size and try again.

It then creates the assurance contract pledge by adding the SIGHASH_ANYONECANPAY OP code to the transaction:

```
Transaction pledge = new Transaction(getParams());
// TODO: Support submitting multiple inputs in a single pledge tx here.
TransactionInput input = pledge.addInput(stub);
project.getOutputs().forEach(pledge::addOutput);
ECKey key = input.getOutpoint().getConnectedKey(this);        checkNotNull(key);
Script script = stub.getScriptPubKey();
if (aesKey != null)
key = key.maybeDecrypt(aesKey);
TransactionSignature signature = pledge.calculateSignature(0, key, script,
Transaction.SigHash.ALL, true /* anyone can pay! */);
if (script.isSentToAddress()) {
input.setScriptSig(ScriptBuilder.createInputScript(signature, key));        }
else if (script.isSentToRawPubKey()) {
// This branch will never be taken with the current design of the app because the
// only way to get money in is via an address, but in future we might support
// direct-to-key payments via the payment protocol.
input.setScriptSig(ScriptBuilder.createInputScript(signature));        }
input.setScriptSig(ScriptBuilder.createInputScript(signature, key));
pledge.setPurpose(Transaction.Purpose.ASSURANCE_CONTRACT_PLEDGE);
log.info("Paid {} satoshis in fees to create pledge tx {}", totalFees, pledge);
```

And that's how the creator implemented his smart contract using the raw Bitcoin protocol. Ugly way of doing things, isn't it? The raw Bitcoin protocol just isn't developer friendly. If you've ever tried using it, you know what I mean. That's why services like chain.com and SDKs that wrap its ugliness will lead the way in terms of developer engagement.

Thus, the money doesn't actually leave your wallet when you make a pledge. It's just part of a signed transaction that hasn't become a valid transaction on the network.

When a user decides to create a project, a BIP70 payment request message is formatted. The outputs are specified normally, and there are only a few things different from the regular payment flow:

- A field labeled title is added. This field sums up the project in a few concise, descriptive words.

- A field labeled image is added. This image contains serialized image bytes that add individuality to the project in the user interface. Hearn had the images be the same aspect ratio as Facebook cover photos so that they are easy to reuse.

- In the case that a `payment_url` is specified, it should speak an extended protocol that permits querying the project status (the current pledges).
- The payment message itself must contain an invalid transaction that only has `SIGHASH_ANYONECANPAYcode>` signatures. Only public, known UTXOs can be spent by the pledge to be considered valid for the project. The memo field can also contain a message from the user (commending the project). Additional fields for contact details are permissible.

After being formatted, the payment message can either be `POST`ed to the `payment_URL` for collection and eventual merging with other pledges, or it can be transferred to the project owner in another way (for example, email). When the owner has it, he can load it into his Lighthouse client. The client provides a GUI for merging pledges and sending the final transaction off to the P2P network.

Bitcoin's scripting language has become more powerful over the years, thanks in large part to the innovations in blockchain technology and Turing-complete smart contract technology coming out of the Ethereum project. It's well suited for most smart contracts, but Turing-complete contracts on the Bitcoin blockchain are an area that is still emerging. Counterparty allows for it, but Counterparty is quite bloated with other unnecessary features. There is, of course, Ethereum itself, but the sidechain code still hasn't been implemented to let you use the Ethereum blockchain with the security of Bitcoin.

Lighthouse is a great case study into the politics that have begun to sink into the Bitcoin protocol. Bitcoin is seven years old and Mike Hearn has been a core developer for almost as long. He submitted about 44 lines of code as a pull request to the Bitcoin core and it was rejected. It was then accepted. Then, later on, it was unmerged after much serious debate. Even with his credentials, he wasn't able to get a simple fix that would build on `OP_SIGHASH_ANYONECANPAY`.

The core developers are very protective of the codebase, and with right purpose—Bitcoin is important fiduciary code and billions of dollars depends on its stability. In that sense, it's the most valuable standalone open source project in existence. There were a total of 167 comments by developers on Hearn's 44-line merge request. He decided instead to create a patch list to implement his "getuxtxo message queries UTXO set, used to check pledges." Hearn even went on to say that Simplified Payment Verification (SPV) wouldn't be possible at this stage in the game because of how much politicking is necessary to make any changes to the core protocol.

This is a good and bad thing: it's good because too many changes could break everything if not carefully analyzed and debated; it's bad because it prevents great changes from becoming part of the core. Sidechains will hopefully solve this problem by allowing for new blockchains for experimentation while still scaffolding the Bitcoin blockchain's security.

Hearn went on to create a protocol called Bitcoin TX for Lighthouse with the patch set that currently has about 16 active nodes.

SPV Wallets

Recall that in the Mikro dapp, we used a third-party API to create and send coins between addresses. Kerala wrapped all the signing and pushing necessary. This is only partially decentralized but a good start. A more decentralized solution is obviously to run the node locally, but the problem with running a Bitcoin node locally is that the blockchain has grown too much. After seven years, downloading and synchronizing the blockchain takes at least four hours and many gigabytes of space. The alternative to this that keeps things decentralized and light is SPV wallets, which is what Hearn implemented using BitcoinJ.

It's possible to build a Bitcoin implementation that does not verify everything, but instead relies on either connecting to a trusted node, or puts its faith in high difficulty as a proxy for proof of validity. BitcoinJ is an implementation of this mode.

In SPV mode, clients can connect to full nodes and download only the block headers. Satoshi described this in his original Bitcoin white paper. Clients can verify that the chain headers connect together properly and that the difficulty is sufficiently high. After that, they request transactions that match certain patterns from a remote node like transactions to your address. This provides copies of those transactions via a Merkle branch linking them to the block in which they appeared. The protocol lets us use the Merkle tree structure to allow for proof of inclusion without needing the entire contents of the block.

SPV allows for even further optimization by discarding block headers that are buried very deep (that is, storage can exclude blocks lower than X headers). If a node is known to be trustworthy, the difficulty no longer matters. If you just want to pick a node at random, the cost to mine a block sequence that has a bogus transaction by an attacker should be higher than the value gained by defrauding you. By changing how low the block has to be, we can exchange confirmation time versus cost of an attack.

Identity

```
public String signAsOwner(PledgingWallet wallet, String message, @Nullable
KeyParameter aesKey)
{
DeterministicKey realKey =
  wallet.getAuthKeyFromIndexOrPubKey(authKey, authKeyIndex);
 if (realKey == null || (aesKey == null && realKey.isEncrypted()))
return null;
return realKey.signMessage(message, aesKey);
}
```

Each project gets its own auth key. The auth key is just a regular Bitcoin secp256k1 key. It's stored in the user's wallet and derived from their HD key hierarchy. Currently, the project uses it solely to prove to the server that the user is the original project creator. The key could also be used to provide messages signed by the creator and prove that a newer version of the project file is legitimate in the future.

The author also has a BitcoinJ template that he's created that's pretty easy to use. You can find it on GitHub (*https://github.com/bitcoinj/wallet-template*).

Figure 5-4 is a great example of a well-designed wallet interface. Basically, it's an SPV wallet written by using BitcoinJ with a default HTML/CSS template scheme setup that you can build on to create your own decentralized application. It's not ideal, because it's not using a metacoin, so it will be difficult if not impossible for you to make money off of whatever you create, but it's a start. There also exists an SPV colored coins wallet called ChromaWallet, but it doesn't have the pretty starter template that this BitcoinJ template has. Combining the template element of BitcoinJ with it would be a really useful tool to have, and I predict someone is going to create it sooner or later.

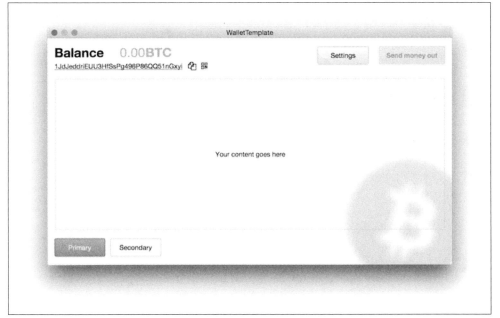

Figure 5-4. Your wallet balance

## CHAPTER 6

La'Zooz

What Is La'Zooz?

Ride sharing applications have taken the world by storm over the past few years. Uber and Lyft are two of the biggest, and Uber seems to be intent on world domination. Uber raked in 2 billion dollars in 2014 alone and is one of the fastest growing startups in the world. The premise is simple: take advantage of the ubiquity of smart phones to let users hail a ride from anywhere, to anywhere. Uber decentralizes the power of the taxi industry by making it possible for anyone to become a driver. Further, it lets anyone call a ride from anywhere with the push of a button using the phone's GPS technology. With the advent of Uber, people are no longer forced to wait for a taxi to drive by, and drivers don't need to wander until a rider is available. Uber provides a matching service and apparently decentralizes it. P2P technology at its finest.

Or is it? Several scandals have emerged out of Uber's corporate culture as of late. Uber has become notorious both for its business practices, and for what it incentivizes and allows its drivers to do. Uber executive Emil Michael told the company to dig up dirt on a particular critical female reporter as well as other opponents. The power the company exerts over its drivers has grown from surveillance into possibly predatory lending practices. Uber's "God Mode," the ability to see all rides happening in any location in real time with all social data attached to each rider, has been the subject of controversy on multiple occasions. Drivers, meanwhile, have been known to hail Lyft cabs only to cancel them, so that riders would instead choose Uber.

Despite these concerns, Uber has grown at an exponential rate over the past few years and is showing revenue numbers in the billions. It provides a useful service: people prefer using a location-aware app to hail a ride over calling a taxi, and it's safe to say the demand for real-time ride-sharing isn't going away anytime soon. But privacy invasion and the vast imbalance of power between a billion-dollar corporation and its contractors are the negatives of Uber that riders must accept when they use its service.

Riders will be able to spend Zooz tokens to get rides from La'Zooz drivers. Drivers have a different app that lets them "mine" Zooz just for driving around. La'Zooz implements what they call a proof-of-movement algorithm. It uses GPS triangulation data to track whether the driver is driving. If they are driving, they'll be able to mine Zooz currency.

Distribution Protocol

So how are the Zooz tokens going to be distributed? We know that drivers are rewarded with Zooz tokens that will be mined as they drive. The amount that they are rewarded for mining decreases with time, similar to the Bitcoin network. This curve, shown in Figure 6-1, has proven to work as an incentive for miners.

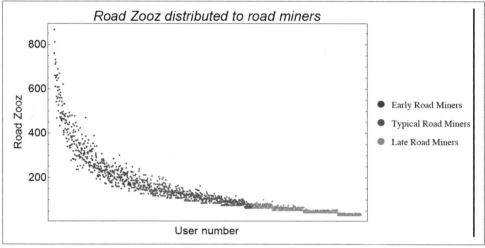

Figure 6-1. La'Zooz tokens

The team has created a community roadmap. The roadmap is a timeline of all future milestones in the La'Zooz project to hit in terms of development, marketing, and overall growth. They believe that early adopters should be rewarded more than late adopters and that people should be rewarded for referring others to the network.

The team decided to have two rounds of a presale to raise funds for the development of the project. This is the equivalent to raising a seed round to develop a prototype before going public via social media and blogs with the launch of your product. They've set up a multisignature coinbase vault that requires two out of three signatures to release the funds. The vault is just a multisig Bitcoin address to which anyone can send funds. If two of the three signers agree to release the funds, the funds are released to whomever sent the money.

The multisig is used as a smart contract that crowd sale buyers can send Bitcoin to and receive Zooz tokens in proportion to the amount they paid. Here are the three possible signers:

- A trusted member of the Bitcoin community
- An independent professional auditor
- A La'Zooz development community representative

As to how these people will be selected and by whom, this is still in the decision process. Eight percent of all the tokens sold during the crowd sale will be issued to all the presale buyers as a bonus. Why this number and why reissue funds at the crowd sale instead of just giving them a bonus for participating early on? It doesn't make sense and it's confusing.

A problem arises if there are many drivers in a region, but no riders; the same problem arises in the opposite situation. This is referred to classically as "the chicken and the egg" problem. La'Zooz aims to counteract it by using an algorithm to detect when there are a certain number of drivers in a particular region. If the number of drivers in the region reaches a certain threshold, the rider app will be activated and riders will only then be able to start requesting rides. This means that the app will be introduced region by region, just like Uber, and full deployment is decided programmatically rather than manually.

DAO Structure

La'Zooz aims to be a community-run network, meaning that there is no difference between creators and the users. Everyone who uses La'Zooz belongs to the same DAO. There is an end of the month vote during which members decide the weight of each member's vote and the reward for each member in the community. Each member can only vote on voting weights for other members who they know (web of trust) as well as the amount of dividend that they receive.

The new weights are calculated on a mixed basis; 75 percent of the input comes from the new vote and 25 percent from the previous month's vote. These are arbitrary numbers and can be tweaked, but it would be better, in my opinion, if it were allocated entirely to the new vote. Creating a DAO is a relatively new experience, and the easier you can make it for members to understand how to participate and exactly how your organizational processes work, the more likely your DAO will be successful. Each member must write down the work that they have done for the benefit of the network at the end of each month before the voting day. The members who vote on others can see their self-described track record and judge the significance on it.

There is never an obligation to vote, which is a good thing. Keep voting opt-in and members won't feel pressured to act a certain way; if they do, they might leave for a freer DAO. Creating community guidelines is a practice in balancing rigidity and freedom and doing so at first in a centralized way to get an initial document out there as fast as possible (creating a team), and then collaboratively as the community adds to it.

La'Zooz went ahead and put out a collaborative white paper (*http://www.lazooz.org/whitepaper.html*) that describes their distribution mechanism, some of the math behind their distribution algorithm, their roadmap, and their vision. Ever since Satoshi released Bitcoin with an accompanying white paper, people who make a dapp tend to publish one as well. To add to the white-paper craze, several high-profile venture capitalists like David Johnson actually promote the use of publishing a white paper as the "right" way to release a dapp. I disagree. The right way to launch a dapp is to provide a real value proposition—something that no centralized competitor could accomplish—and explain it in the simplest way possible, using methods with which most people are familiar.

If that means a landing page for the information, a forum for your community with voting capabilities integrated, and an explainer video for your dapp, so be it. White papers are not necessary and can actually cause unnecessary confusion if all of your dapp's related information is centralized into it, as is the case with La'Zooz. A white paper doesn't have to double as a business plan, member roles, and everything else associated with your organization.

Be that as it may, the La'Zooz team went ahead and created a nonprofit legal organization in Israel to make sure they were cleared with the state. Every member in the community is rewarded and has a weighted vote on how the app moves forward, but the team itself forms the legal organization. A certain percentage of dividends will go to them during the reward phase at the end of the month, just like everyone else. Interestingly, they've stipulated in their by-laws to be legally contractually obliged to follow the orders of the community vote with the funds that they receive.

In this way, the DAO establishes itself as a liquid democracy. Everyone has a vote, voting is opt-in and delegated by weight, yet the creators are still represented. The representatives take care of most of the organizational complexity, but if at any point the community feels that they are corrupt or lack the necessary leadership to maintain and grow the network, they can propose and vote in a new set of representatives.

The reward mechanism described in the paper is murky and still in development. Giving people rewards for their work should come in the form of dividends. Internal currencies don't offer liquidity at the outset; they only gain it as the network grows. We can think of internal tokens as shares in the network. A smart contract could be written to give a dividend out to every public-private keypair that holds Zooz tokens.

The dividend would be proportional to the amount of tokens that the address held. An altcoin called bitshares created by Dan Larimer uses a consensus algorithm called Delegated Proof of Stake that functions similarly. Whereas Zooz tokens could be thought of as shares in the La'Zooz DAO as well as an internal currency, the dividends could be in Bitcoin or just more Zooz. Bitcoins are more liquid, but Zooz have more potential for value. This is for the creator to decide, but I think Bitcoin would be nice to have as a dividend.

UX

Let's take a look at some of the designs that La'Zooz has created. Decentralized apps thus far haven't exactly had award-winning frontend interfaces, but La'Zooz seems to understand the importance of great design.

Upon starting the mining app, the user sees a greeting and is taken to a page of their metrics. Figures 6-2 and 6-3 show some of the dummy metrics included in the test version of the app. The app is meant to be run as a background process with all the mining happening while the user is driving; they can even have other apps up in the foreground while they are mining.

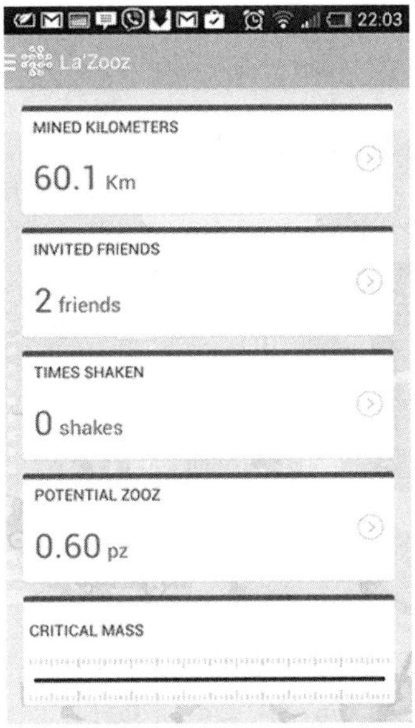

Figure 6-2. La'Zooz Stats

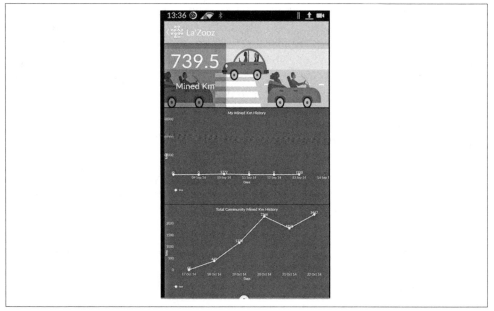

Figure 6-3. Graph of Mined Coins

The driver is able to view her current Zooz balance (Figure 6-4) by clicking the icon in the sidebar. The Zooz app doubles as a wallet for her currency. She can use the QR code and export functionality to send and receive currency in real life to other people or businesses. The potential Zooz balance is an interesting marker. The app calculates how much a driver could run if she continues mining for whatever the time to next block is. What is the Sybil-prevention mechanism here? How does La'Zooz prevent a user from spinning up multiple instances of the mining process to earn more coins than they should by posing to be multiple users simultaneously? We'll need to dive into the codebase (*https://github.com/laZooz/lbm-client*) to see this functionality.

Architecture

Data storage and retrieval

We saw in our Mikro dapp that a DHT was used to store data and a BitTorrent transfer protocol was used to retrieve data. This was made possible by using IPFS, a culmination of both technologies. In OpenBazaar, a DHT was used as well but didn't have replication built in, so it wasn't as robust. If a node goes offline and no one views their data beforehand, that data goes offline, as well.

Figure 6-4. Zooz balance

In Lighthouse, the developer didn't even attempt to use a decentralized data store because it was too difficult to implement. Instead, projects were broadcast over the Web and project files were shared and downloaded by participants to load into their instance of Lighthouse. So, how does La'Zooz deal with data? Well, we can see that there is a file named ServerComs in the source code. Server communication? That doesn't sound very decentralized. Let's take a look at three methods in that class:

```
public void registerToServer(String cellphone)
    {
        String url = StaticParms.BASE_SERVER_URL + "api_register";

        List<NameValuePair> params = new ArrayList<NameValuePair>();
        params.add(new BasicNameValuePair("cellphone", cellphone ));

        this.postRequestToServer(-1, -1, url, params);

    }

public void
    setLocation1dddsfsdfs(String UserId, String UserSecret, String data)
    {
        String url = StaticParms.BASE_SERVER_URL + "api_set_location";

        List<NameValuePair> params = new ArrayList<NameValuePair>();
        params.add(new BasicNameValuePair("user_id", UserId ));
        params.add(new BasicNameValuePair("user_secret", UserSecret ));
```

```
        params.add(new BasicNameValuePair("location_list", data ));
        this.postRequestToServer(-1, -1, url, params);
    }

    public void getUserKeyData(String UserId, String UserSecret)
    {
        String url = StaticParms.BASE_SERVER_URL + "api_get_user_key_data";
        List<NameValuePair> params = new ArrayList<NameValuePair>();
        params.add(new BasicNameValuePair("user_id", UserId ));
        params.add(new BasicNameValuePair("user_secret", UserSecret ));
        this.postRequestToServer(-1, -1, url, params);
    }
```

So, it seems like these three methods are getting user data, setting user location, and registering a user account with a server, respectively. And what is that BASE_SERVER_URL variable? Well in the class StaticParams, we find it defined:

```
public static final String BASE_SERVER_URL = "https://client.laZooz.org/";
```

It turns out that it's storing and retrieving data from a central server. As someone who has been studying dapps for a while, I'm not surprised that much. There is so much noise in this space; projects can be really loud and have a lot of hype, followers, and promise, and it ends up that they cut corners on issues as critical as data storage. It could be for lack of finding great decentralized storage tools like IPFS, or just a lack of knowledge of how things should be done in a dapp to keep it sufficiently decentralized. The fact that user data is stored on a server makes the app similar to Uber, other than the fact that it's using an internal currency and has a co-op-like structure, rather than a corporate one. There is an Android wrapper for IPFS that La'Zooz could have implemented. You can find it at *https://github.com/dylanPowers/ipfs-android*.

Coins

So, what blockchain is La'Zooz using to issue its internal currency called Zooz?

```
    protected String doInBackground(String... params) {

            ServerCom bServerCom = new ServerCom(MainActivity.this);
            JSONObject jsonReturnObj=null;
            try {
                MySharedPreferences msp = MySharedPreferences.getInstance();
        bServerCom.getUserKeyData(msp.getUserId(MainActivity.this),
msp.getUserSecret(MainActivity.this));
                jsonReturnObj = bServerCom.getReturnObject();
            } catch (Exception e1) {
                e1.printStackTrace();
            }
            String serverMessage = "";
            try {
                if (jsonReturnObj == null)
                    serverMessage = "ConnectionError";
                else {
```

```
serverMessage = jsonReturnObj.getString("message");
if (serverMessage.equals("success")){
    String ZoozBalance =
jsonReturnObj.getString("Zooz_balance");
```

The method is asking the server for the wallet balance. That means that the wallet is hosted on their server instead of being hosted locally. Strike two for the centralization! It's not a third-party wallet host, it's La'Zooz's own server. As for the type of blockchain it is using, because it's on their server there is no client-side code we can dive into, but I do know that they are using the Mastercoin blockchain from what they've stated on various social media outlets.

Mastercoin is a layer on top of the Bitcoin blockchain. It inserts data into the blockchain via transactions and, from the standpoint of the Bitcoin miners, this data is meaningless. Unlike Bitcoin or any altcoin that relies on its own blockchain, Mastercoin is incapable of acting like a smart contract engine. Anyone could double-spend Mastercoins from a given address. Nothing will stop someone from publishing conflicting Mastercoin transactions on the blockchain, and the only thing the Mastercoin protocol does is define a rule by which a single transaction is ignored.

That's not all. Some of La'Zooz's features require its users to participate actively, but there is nothing in the protocol that asks them to behave correctly. A good example is that the Mastercoin protocol has a feature called "register a data stream," in which the owner of a Bitcoin address can declare that they'll be publishing data hidden in transactions from it. The owner could pledge to post the price of gasoline every week to that stream. However, there isn't really anything required by him to post data on a regular schedule. More important, there is nothing preventing him from lying. This flaw makes the entire datastream valueless as an input for smart contracts.

Unlike Mastercoin, colored coins insert very minimal data on the blockchain, so they're much lighter for miners. Smart contracts can be created using Bitcoin's internal scripting system or by using a sidechain that utilizes Turing-complete contract creation.

Contracts

At this point we've found that data is centralized on their server as well as the wallet node that connects to the Mastercoin network. Smart contracts would allow for an automated crowd sale, and they said they are using a coinbase multisig vault to release funds. But what about paying dividends? Automated escrow payments are the hallmark of smart contracts. The contract would live in the blockchain and, seeing how they are using the Bitcoin blockchain with the Mastercoin protocol, surely they must be using the Bitcoin scripting language to make their smart contracts. A quick look on the Ethereum home page leads us to find that La'Zooz is one of the projects using Ethereum for smart contracts.

Ethereum is great and their tools for building smart contracts are more mature than Bitcoin's, but the fact of the matter is that their blockchain is unproven to work and they are going to have to massively reduce in size or spend forever playing "security whack-a-mole," as Gavin Andresen (lead developer of Bitcoin) puts it. At its best, when the sidechain protocol is released, Ethereum will become a sidechain to Bitcoin, and if someone really needs to write Turing-complete contracts, they can, without being exposed to the risk of relying on the Ethereum blockchain to be secure with their internal currency. Using the Ethereum blockchain in the meantime is just not smart development if you want your dapp to be profitable.

Improvements

La'Zooz is an ambitious startup. It is trying to create the first DAO that involves a distributed workforce that receives dividends, has votes, and ties in with the existing legal infrastructure. It could just be using centralized data, wealth, and identity as a placeholder in its development stage. As for right now, although its intentions seem good enough, it seems to be placing itself at risk for the possibility of not one but several points of failure.

La'Zooz should use the colored-coins protocol to issue assets. Zooz tokens should be used as both shares in the network and as a currency. Dividends would be received by creating a smart contract to give all people in the network the dividends proportional to their stake in the network. The actual Zooz app could be an SPV wallet for colored coins for total decentralization, but if it wanted to use a web wallet for ease of development, it could use Coinprism.

The way La'Zooz structured its DAO is commendable. If it has legal contracts requiring those who are listed under the by-laws of its company in Israel to obey the will of the community vote, it has avoided the legal limbo associated with a DAO by complying with local regulation and sticking to the principles of decentralization via liquid democracy. Voting should happen in app as a feature that is just a tab on the sidebar.

Users should opt in to vote; anyone can submit a proposal for a feature request, new regions to focus marketing on, or leadership change. Anyone should be allowed to vote on those proposals. The voting forum would work Reddit-style, with the best votes being moved up to the top. The leadership or representatives of the DAO listed under the by-laws would enact these proposals, as they would legally be required.

The data should not be centralized, but that's a given. A data storage and retrieval service that utilizes a DHT should be used like IPFS. Having a server on which the team can own all the data defeats the purpose of decentralization, although in the case of La'Zooz it might be a little different because it is legally bound to do only what the community wants. The community will most likely demand complete transparency. That transparency means none of its data can be sold to any third-party source without the community's permission. Doing so would be illegal.

Jobs in the La'Zooz DAO should be either role-specific or full stack. Full stack professions are already emerging in the startup sector, but in the case of a DAO, full stack must mean not just in terms of engineering, but in terms of playing different roles throughout the company. That includes marketing, engineering, and customer relations. Hiring, reviewing, and firing employees in a decentralized way can be difficult. There should be no barrier to enter the DAO, and the review process is something La'Zooz has spoken about (voting on member rewards and voting weights). Firing could come up as a proposal by a disgruntled member.

Firing should essentially be the equivalent of banning someone in a distributed manner. A bad actor could be trying to DDoS the network or attempting to upload child porn. People should vote on firing the member (those who knew the member) and then the representatives in the DAO would ban that person's address by implementing a blacklist in the blockchain stored locally on all nodes. That means if an address was on a blacklist, they would not be able to transact with any of the other nodes on the network. The blacklist would be stored in the blockchain so that all nodes could agree on it.

La'Zooz shouldn't use Ethereum for smart contracts until the sidechain proposal is ready. The Bitcoin scripting language, though not fully Turing-complete, can handle most use cases that involve escrowing automatic payments.

Finally, La'Zooz shouldn't concatenate all the instructions for its DAO into one white paper. Instead, it should modularize the data into many different easy-to-read parts for the layperson. It should be easy to find as well because web pages are more Google-friendly than PDFs.

Conclusion

This tour of a few dapps-in-progress should give you a few thoughts to springboard from as you develop your own. Be guided by the twin watchwords of *openness* and *decentralization*, and you will not go wrong.

Index

About the Author

Siraj Raval is a dapp developer, entrepreneur, and a technical storyteller at heart. He's a full-time YouTube star on his show, Sirajology. He is founder of a crowdfunding platform for developers called Havi, has developed several iOS apps including Meetup, and has worked on a host of open source work. Besides being a programmer, Siraj is also a traveler, musician, postmodernist, and scuba diver.

Colophon

The animal on the cover of *Decentralized Applications* is the silver roughy (*Hoplostethus mediterraneus*), also known as the Mediterranean slimehead.

This deep-sea fish is widespread throughout the Atlantic and Western Indian Oceans at depths ranging from 100 to 1,175 meters. The silver roughy is small, reaching just 42 centimeters, with an oblong shape, large eyes, and a forked tail.

Silver roughy fish have been known to live up to 11 years. Their diet consists mainly of crustaceans.

Many of the animals on O'Reilly covers are endangered; all of them are important to the world. To learn more about how you can help, go to *animals.oreilly.com*.

The cover image is from the Dover Pictorial Archive. The cover fonts are URW Typewriter and Guardian Sans. The text font is Adobe Minion Pro; the heading font is Adobe Myriad Condensed; and the code font is Dalton Maag's Ubuntu Mono.

Get even more for your money.

Join the O'Reilly Community, and register the O'Reilly books you own. It's free, and you'll get:

- $4.99 ebook upgrade offer
- 40% upgrade offer on O'Reilly print books
- Membership discounts on books and events
- Free lifetime updates to ebooks and videos
- Multiple ebook formats, DRM FREE
- Participation in the O'Reilly community
- Newsletters
- Account management
- 100% Satisfaction Guarantee

Signing up is easy:

1. Go to: oreilly.com/go/register
2. Create an O'Reilly login.
3. Provide your address.
4. Register your books.

Note: English-language books only

To order books online:
oreilly.com/store

For questions about products or an order:
orders@oreilly.com

To sign up to get topic-specific email announcements and/or news about upcoming books, conferences, special offers, and new technologies:
elists@oreilly.com

For technical questions about book content:
booktech@oreilly.com

To submit new book proposals to our editors:
proposals@oreilly.com

O'Reilly books are available in multiple DRM-free ebook formats. For more information:
oreilly.com/ebooks

- Could we make it so that you get paid a tiny amount of money when someone reads you? Basically good twaddlers would find themselves remunerated. Or some similar system.
- You should need to pay a small token sum (to me!) to register a user. Maybe an Ethereum smart contract can enforce this?
- Is it possible to have an other tmp escrow system? You can create a username, you will only own it after you've mined a bit (or payed); otherwise it's redrawn. Actually, this could be done without escrow, just limiting the risk by maxing on the number of people in limbo at any given time.